The Treasury of

ENGLISH
CHURCH
MUSIC

General Editors: GERALD H. KNIGHT and WILLIAM L. REED

The Treasury of
ENGLISH

BLANDFORD PRESS : LONDON

CHURCH MUSIC

MUSIC

Volume TWO 1545 – 1650

Edited by PETER LE HURAY

THE LIBRARY
GARRETT-EVANGELICAL
THEOLOGICAL SEMINARY
EVANSTON, ILLINOIS

FIRST PUBLISHED IN 1965
© BLANDFORD PRESS LIMITED
167 HIGH HOLBORN, LONDON, W.C.1

LIBRARY OF CONGRESS
CATALOGUE NUMBER 65-25006

MUSIC LAYOUT BY R. T. MATTHEWS AND ENGRAVED BY
LOWE & BRYDONE (PRINTERS) LTD., VICTORIA ROAD, LONDON, N.W.10
FILMSET IN BASKERVILLE BY BOOKPRINT LIMITED, CRAWLEY, SUSSEX.
PRINTED IN GREAT BRITAIN BY LOWE & BRYDONE (PRINTERS) LTD. AND
BOUND BY RICHARD CLAY (THE CHAUCER PRESS) LTD., BUNGAY, SUFFOLK.

THE LIBRARY
SEABURY-WESTERN
THEOLOGICAL SEMINARY
EVANSTON, ILLINOIS

M1999
.T78
v. 2

GENERAL EDITORS' PREFACE

IT is perhaps not unreasonable to state that no other country possesses so fine and unbroken a choral tradition as England, and to claim that English Church music at its best compares with the finest to be found anywhere in the world.

Like the householder in the Gospel, the editors have sought to bring forth out of this 'treasure, things new and old', from the earliest experiments in polyphony to the challenging compositions of today, and in the compilation of the first three volumes they have been assisted by eminent musicians, each of whom is a specialist in his own field.

Volume 1, which covers the earliest period to the Reformation, is edited by Denis Stevens.

Volume 2, representing the 'golden age' from the Reformation until the death of Charles I, is edited by Peter le Huray.

Volume 3, containing works from the early days of the Commonwealth to the accession of George III, is edited by Christopher Dearnley.

Much of the material in the above volumes is published for the first time, and a number of well-known pieces appear in newly-edited versions.

Volume 4 covers the period from 1760 to 1900, and includes an introduction by George Guest.

Volume 5 contains the works of twentieth-century composers (British, Canadian, Australian, and American) and includes an introduction by David Lumsden.

It is hoped that this publication will stimulate all who have an interest in Church Music to explore further the treasures that exist. What is of even greater importance, it is hoped that choirs throughout the world will be encouraged to sing this music worthily to the glory of God, for their own inspiration and that of very many others who listen to it.

GERALD H. KNIGHT
WILLIAM L. REED

The title page of John Day's *Certaine notes*, 1565
(British Museum)

VI

CONTENTS

* also ascribed to JOHN HILTON the Elder (before 1565–after 1612)

ACKNOWLEDGMENTS

THE editor wishes to thank Mr. Jeremy Noble and Mr. John Morehen for invaluable help in the preparation of this volume, and the Librarians of the following Institutions for permission to consult manuscripts in their possession:

> University of California
> Pembroke College, Cambridge
> Peterhouse, Cambridge
> Durham Cathedral
> Ely Cathedral
> Gloucester Cathedral
> British Museum, London
> Lambeth Palace, London
> Royal College of Music, London
> New York Public Library
> Bodleian Library, Oxford
> Christ Church Library, Oxford
> St. Michael's College, Tenbury
> York Minster

Acknowledgment is also due to those publishers who have given permission for the inclusion of copyright material as indicated at the foot of the music pages.

PETER LE HURAY
St. Catharine's College
Cambridge 1965

Tenor C

Tenor Cantoris.

THE
FIRST BOOK
OF SELECTED
CHVRCH MVSICK,

Confiſting of Services and Anthems, ſuch as are
now uſed in the Cathedrall, and Collegiat Churches
of this Kingdome. Never before Printed.

Whereby ſuch Bookes as were heretofore with much diffi-
culty and Charges, tranſcribed for the uſe of the Quire,
are now to the ſaving of much Labour and expence, publiſht for the
generall good of all ſuch as ſhall deſire them either for publick
or private exerciſe.

Collected out of divers approved Authors, by IOHN BARNARD
one of the Minor Cannons of the Cathedrall Church
of Saint *Paul*, London.

Pſalme 47. Verſe 6. 7.
O Sing praiſes, ſing praiſes unto (our) God: O ſing praiſes, ſing praiſes unto our King.
For God is King of all the earth : Sing ye praiſes with underſtanding.

Pſalme 150. Verſe 4.
Praiſe him with ſtringed Inſtruments and Organs.

LONDON,
Printed by EDWARD GRIFFEN, and are to be ſold
at the Signe of the three *Lutes* in *Pauls* Alley. 1641.

The title page of John Barnard's *First Book of Selected Church Musick*, 1641
(By courtesy of the Dean and Chapter, Lichfield Cathedral)

INTRODUCTION

FOR some years before the first Act of Uniformity became law the question of liturgical reform had been very much in the air. As early as 1537 Archbishop Cranmer and Thomas Cromwell were at work on proposals for a revised Breviary, and in 1539 an authorised translation of the Bible was published by royal command. At that time, however, the possibility of establishing a wholly vernacular liturgy does not appear to have been seriously considered. A contemporary diarist did indeed record that an English version of Te Deum had been sung at meetings of a radical group called 'the new sect' in London, and it was rumoured that an English form of Mass had been celebrated on more than one occasion in villages to the north-east of London. It was not until 1544, however, that Henry VIII sanctioned the first major change in the direction of a vernacular liturgy, the replacement of the Latin Procession, *in causa necessitas*, with an English equivalent. By this time it was clear that the King—a conservative in liturgical matters—had gone far to accepting one of the basic premises of the Reformation, namely that the laity had a right and duty to take a full part in public worship. It was doubtless with this in mind that Cranmer wrote his oft-quoted letter to the King on the subject of processional music, in which he urged the need for clarity and simplicity.

There was indeed a general feeling that a disproportionate amount of time and effort had in the past been expended on music: as Erasmus put it, 'They chant nowadays in our churches in what is an unknown tongue and nothing else, while you will not hear a sermon once in six months telling people to amend their lives. Modern church music is so constructed that the congregation cannot hear a single word clearly, and the choristers themselves do not understand what they are singing. . . .'

The next steps in the process of liturgical reformation were not taken until 1547. In May of that year, just four months after the coronation of Edward VI, an English form of Compline was tried out at the Chapel Royal, and, during the course of Mass held at Westminster Abbey in November to mark the opening of Parliament and Convocation, the Kyrie, Gloria, Creed, Sanctus and Agnus Dei were sung in English. Early in the following year English versions of Matins, Communion and Evensong came into use at St. Paul's Cathedral and also at some of the more progressive city churches. Six months later Parliament considered and approved *An Act for the uniformity of service and admini-*

stration of the sacraments throughout the realm, and in June 1549 the first *Book of Common Prayer* became the one official service book of the church in England.

This did not by any means mark the end of the liturgical reformation, however, for a second *Act of Uniformity* followed not three years later, together with a much revised prayer book. That there can have been any real uniformity of religious practices and beliefs during these turbulent years is much to be doubted. As Martin Bucer, the Regius Professor of Divinity at Cambridge, observed to the King in a letter of December 1551, too much had been attempted with too little preparation:

> Your sacred majesty has already found by experience how grave are the evils which ensued on taking away by force false worship from your people, without sufficient preliminary instruction. . . . Some have on this account made horrible sedition, others have raised perilous dissensions in the state, and to this very day wherever they can, either cause new trouble or increase what has been excited. Some turn the prescribed forms of prayer into mere papistical abuse, and although these are now in the vulgar tongue the 'sacrificers' recite it of set purpose so indistinctly that it cannot be understood, whilst the people altogether refuse to understand or listen. . . .

During these early years several composers of considerable stature were writing for the English Church, including Christopher Tye and Thomas Tallis, both well on in middle age, Thomas Caustun and Robert Parsons, John Shepherd, probably in his thirties, and William Mundy, a young man of little more than twenty. All but Parsons were then members of the Chapel Royal. Altogether some fifty or so attributable compositions of various kinds can be dated to the Edwardian period. Most of these are by Chapel Royal musicians, but there are a few by provincial and unknown composers, notably John Brimley of Durham, John Heath, Robert Johnson, Osbert Parsley of Norwich, and John Thorne of York. There are also a large number of anonymous compositions in the two major Edwardian sources, Bodleian MSS. Mus.sch.e.420-2 and British Museum Roy.App. MSS. 74-6.

Whilst the extant music can represent only a very small part of the original Edwardian repertory, enough has survived to show how wide was the range of forms and styles then in current use: the simple monodic chant (see page 7), the homophonic chant—the precursor of the late seventeenth-century anglican chant (see page 8), the short four-part anthem (see page 46), the rather more elaborate polyphonic anthem (see page 22), and—most complex of all—the festal 'Great Service', developed by Tallis, Shepherd, Robert Parsons (see page 33), and William Mundy.

The unexpected accession of Mary Tudor to the throne in 1553 led to the temporary restoration of full communion with Rome. During the short-lived Marian reaction composers once again made use of late-medieval techniques of cantus firmus composition, and it must have been then that William Mundy and Robert White (see page 50) wrote most of their music for the Sarum rites.

With the death of Mary in 1558 the *status quo* of 1552 was gradually restored, though (at Elizabeth's insistence apparently) with small and highly controversial modifications. Above all, the severe ornaments rubric of the 1552 Prayer Book affecting the use of vestments was replaced by one permitting and indeed requiring a return to the position that had been established in 1549. In a very real sense, of course, music was a liturgical 'ornament', and as such it was a very live issue in the Vestarian Controversy that followed. Many influential divines were against the use of non-congregational music of any kind, and during the 1562 session of Convocation a motion was discussed, urging the complete abolition of organs and 'curious singing'. The motion was defeated, but among the sponsors, significantly enough, were the Deans of Exeter, Hereford, Lichfield, Oxford and St. Paul's, and the proctors of the Deans and Chapters of Gloucester, Rochester, Westminster Abbey and Winchester. And as the Vestarian Controversy widened into an attack upon the episcopal system itself the Reformers became increasingly critical of 'cathedral' music.

To what extent musicians were hampered in their work by the puritanism of the early-Elizabethan church is an open question. There can be no doubt, however, that inflation and inadequate stipends were mainly responsible for a decline in musical standards during the later part of the sixteenth century. As the composer and writer Thomas Whythorne observed:

> [music is] so slenderly maintained in the cathedral churches and colleges and parish churches, that when the old store of musicians be worn out which were bred when the music of the church was maintained (which is like to be in a short time) you shall have a few or none remaining. . .
>
> [Autobiography c. 1575]

Indeed, had it not been for the Chapel Royal the history of English cathedral music might well have been much the poorer. For by cathedral standards Chapel Royal salaries were munificent, whilst the conditions of work were outstandingly good. Moreover the Queen herself took a keen and almost professional interest in the choir. Her successors too, though by no means as musical, were equally concerned that the fine traditions of the Chapel Royal choir should be maintained. It can be no accident, then, that the history of English 'cathedral' music during the late sixteenth and early seventeenth centuries is to a very large extent the history of the Chapel Royal. Tallis, Robert Parsons, William Mundy, Byrd, Morley, Bull, Thomas Tomkins and Orlando Gibbons were all members of the Chapel choir: Thomas Weelkes, the one 'provincial' composer of unquestioned stature, had certainly the expectation of a place in the Chapel choir, even if he did not in fact secure it.

To some extent at least the very early compositions for the English rites must be regarded as experimental. Imitative points are in general rather rigidly developed and the melodic motives used in these points conform closely to easily imitable archetypes. In the finest music of the later periods this rigidity is gone. The melodic lines of Byrd's Nunc dimittis, for example, (see page 64) have a much greater relevance to the text than do those of the earlier 'Great Service' setting by Parsons; the rhythms are considerably more varied, and the melodic shapes are far more arresting. There is, also, a sense of tonal direction in the later work that is completely lacking in the earlier. These new qualities are even more apparent in the large-scale polyphonic anthems of the late sixteenth and early seventeenth centuries, of which Byrd's *Sing joyfully* (see page 77), Tomkins's *Arise, O Lord* (see page 143) and Weelkes's *Gloria in excelsis* (see page 154) are outstanding examples.

By the end of the sixteenth century, too, a new technique of composition had come to full maturity, involving the use of solo voices and instruments, as well as full choir. The earliest compositions in the 'verse' style are by composers of the Chapel Royal, Richard Farrant (?-1581), William Mundy (*c.* 1530–1591) and William Byrd (1543–1623). Mundy's *Ah, helpless wretch* (see page 28) is very typical of the new form, in its succession of solos and choruses, and in its short instrumental interludes. Mundy here shows a new awareness of melody as an 'expressive' agent in musical composition, as do Morley and Weelkes in their superb settings of *Out of the deep* (see page 114) and *Give ear, O Lord* (see page 166).

The search for ever more direct forms of expression led to the rapid disintegration of the polyphonic style during the early years of the seventeenth century. The process of disintegration is already apparent in Gibbons's verse music, and especially in the remarkable setting of *See, see the Word is incarnate*—one of his finest compositions—in which idea follows idea with supreme speed and force. It is to be seen equally in Dering's *Factum est silentium* (see page 175), which is considerably more sectional and varied in texture than are the 'learned' motets of Tallis and Byrd (see pages 14 and 87). From the 1620s, too, elements of the Italian *seconda practica* began to appear in English music. One of the Chapel Royal choirmen, Walter Porter, had for a time studied under Monteverdi, and almost a dozen anthems of his were in the Chapel Royal repertory during the 1630s. Only one of these has survived, unfortunately (see page 232). If this is typical of his other work, however, it is easy to see why his music was so little known, for the highly coloratura treble and tenor solos call for singers of unusual skill and imagination. In a less extreme form, Italianate influences are to be seen in the pre-Restoration music of William Child: the short introit printed at the end of this volume (see page 248) is based on a series of progressions quite unlike those to be found in earlier English liturgical music.

Further development in this direction was abruptly brought to a halt by the outbreak of civil war. In the spring of 1642 King Charles I was confronted at Oxford with certain 'Propositions for Peace', one of which urged 'the taking away of all archbishops, bishops, and their chancellors and prebendaries, and all vicars choral and choristers. . . .' Although Charles then refused his assent he could do nothing when the Long Parliament took steps two years later to abolish both the episcopal system and the Book of Common Prayer. By the summer of 1647 choral services everywhere had been stopped, in many cases to the accompaniment of much desecration and destruction. These were indeed sad times. But to those Puritans who were in close touch with the Almighty there was great cause for rejoicing; for at last, in place of 'roaring boys', 'tooting and squeaking organ pipes', and 'the cathedral catches of Morley' was set up 'a most blessed, orthodox preaching ministry'. Godliness and righteousness had prevailed, at last!

CALENDAR OF EVENTS

c. 1500–10	Tye, Tallis and Merbecke born.
c. 1520–30	Shepherd and William Mundy born.
1521	Death of Fayrfax.
1534	'An Act concerning the King's Highness to be Supreme Head of the Church of England and to have authority to reform and redress all errors, heresies and abuses in the same'.
1536–40	The dissolution of the monasteries.
1536	Injunctions issued requiring that copies of the Bible, both in Latin and English, be placed in every parish church 'for every man that will to look and read thereon'.
c. 1539	Myles Coverdale's *Goostly psalmes and spiritual songs*, published on the model of the Lutheran 'geistliche Gesenge': the collection was subsequently banned by Henry VIII.
1543	Byrd born.
1544	Cranmer's English Litany published and authorized for general use.
1545	Death of Taverner.
1547	February 20th, Coronation of Edward VI.
	May: an English form of Compline sung by the choir of the Chapel Royal.
	November: at the service marking the opening of Parliament and Convocation, the Ordinary of the Mass sung in English.
1547–48	Restrictions imposed upon the use of florid Latin music.
1548	March: sections of the Mass translated into English and published by authority as the *Order of the Communion*.
	May: services at St. Paul's and at some of the London parish churches first said and sung in English.

1549 'An Act for the uniformity of service and the administration of the sacraments throughout the realm', following the use of the English *Book of Common Prayer* (first published early in 1549).
Thomas Sternhold's *Certayne Psalmes, chosen out of the Psalter of David and drawn into Englishe metre*, published.

1550 Merbecke's *booke of Common praier noted*, published.

1552 'An Act for the uniformity of common prayer and administration of the sacraments', following the revised *Book of Common Prayer* (1552).

1553 Coronation of Mary Tudor, September.
'An Act for the repeal of certain statutes made in the time of the reign of King Edward VI', restoring 'all such divine service and administration of sacraments as were most commonly used in the realm of England in the last year of the reign of our late sovereign lord King Henry the Eighth. . . .'

1557 Thomas Morley born.

1558 Elizabeth I proclaimed Queen, November 17th.

1559 'An Act for the uniformity of common prayer and divine service in the Church, and the administration of the sacraments', restoring the *Book of Common Prayer* 'so authorized by Parliament in the said fifth and sixth year of the reign of King Edward the Sixth. . . .'

1560 Congregational singing becomes very popular in London and in the provinces, based on the metrical psalter of Sternhold and Hopkins.

1562 Proposals for the abolition of organs and for the ending of 'curious singing' discussed in the Lower House of Convocation, but rejected by a narrow majority.

c. 1563 John Bull born.

1565 John Day's *Certaine notes* published, a collection of Services and anthems; Day had originally intended to bring out this music in 1560.

1570 The Papal Bull against Elizabeth.

1572 Thomas Tomkins born.

c. 1575 Inflation, a serious problem since the early years of the century, results in much unrest and hardship, and the lowering of musical standards. Non-conformist agitation causes the government increasing concern.
Thomas Weelkes born.

1575 The *Cantiones quae ab argumento sacrae vocantur*, published by Byrd and Tallis, organists of the Chapel Royal.

1583 William Whitgift, the new archbishop of Canterbury, introduces measures against separatism and presbyterianism.
Orlando Gibbons born.

1588 The publication of Byrd's *Psalmes, Sonets, & songs of sadnes and pietie* marks the beginning of a very active period of music printing, lasting some thirty years.

1593– The first four books of Hooker's *The Laws of Ecclesiastical Polity* published. During the course of the sixteenth century the cost of living is said to have risen approximately threefold; salaries paid to church musicians were in general no higher than they had been fifty or more years before.

1603 James VI of Scotland crowned King of England, on July 25th.

1604 Salaries of the Gentlemen of the Chapel Royal raised from £30 to £40 per annum.

1605 Discovery of the Gunpowder Plot.
Byrd's first book of *Gradualia* published.

1606 William Child born.

1607 Byrd's second book of *Gradualia* published.

1625 Charles I proclaimed King of England.

1626 William Laud becomes Dean of the Chapel Royal, and during the following two years a Privy Councillor and Bishop of London.

1628 The beginning of the high-church controversy at Durham in which Prebendary Cosin was particularly involved.

1633 William Laud appointed Archbishop of Canterbury; more vigorous measures taken to improve musical standards everywhere; growing unrest at Laud's high-church policies.

1637 Attempts made to impose a new Prayer Book on the Scottish Kirk; this arouses great opposition and the book is withdrawn.

1640 Opening of the 'Long Parliament' on November 3rd.

1641 John Barnard's *First Book of Selected Church Musick* published—the first liturgical collection since Day's *Certaine notes* of 1565.

1644 Abolition of the *Book of Common Prayer*; choral services may have continued in one or two cathedrals for a year or so after this, but by 1647 all cathedral choirs had been disbanded.

1645 William Laud executed.

1649 Charles I executed, on January 30th.

NOTES ON THE MUSIC

CHRISTOPHER TYE: Nunc dimittis.
Christopher Tye took his Mus.B. at Cambridge in 1536; he had then been teaching and composing for more than ten years, and in all probability singing in the choir of King's College, Cambridge. By 1542 he was Master of the Choristers at Ely Cathedral. In 1552 he published a metrical version of chapters from the *Acts of the Apostles*, with music, describing himself on the title page as a Gentleman of the Chapel Royal and dedicating the work to Edward VI. In July, 1560, he was ordained deacon and in the following year he resigned his post at Ely Cathedral to take up the living of Doddington-cum-Marche in the Ely diocese. Nothing is known of him after 1571: a new rector was appointed to the living of Doddington in 1573.

The text of the Nunc dimittis comes from the so-called Marshall Primer of *c.* 1535. During the later years of the reign of Henry VIII several English Primers were published, including 'Marshall's' Primer, Bishop Hilsey's Primer and the King's Primer of 1545. These manuals of private prayer were designed to instruct those who were 'unlearned' in the Latin tongue in the essentials of the Christian faith, and they contained amongst other things translations of the daily office hours—Matins, Lauds, Prime, the Third, Sixth and Ninth Hours, Vespers and Compline. Many musical settings of Primer texts have survived, including this unusual composition by Tye. The extended use of melisma, in particular, suggests an early date. The following are available for comparison: *I will exalt thee*, TCMO 59, OUP 1936; *Praise the Lord, ye children*, ed., A. Ramsbotham, TCMO 58, OUP 1930; and *Christ rising again*, OUP 1966 (probably a late work for the scoring is unusually rich).

JOHN MERBECKE: Nunc dimittis, Communion anthem and Agnus Dei
Soon after the coronation of Edward VI in February 1547, experimental forms of service in English were tried out at the Chapel Royal, Westminster Abbey and St. Paul's Cathedral. Within the space of little more than two years services everywhere were being said and sung in English after the use of the *Book of Common Prayer* (1549):

the use of Latin and Hebrew, however, was permitted at Oxford and Cambridge. The new prayer book contained not a note of music, nor did its rubrics state at all clearly what part music was to have in public worship. In an attempt to remedy these deficiencies, John Merbecke published a year later his *booke of Common praier noted*, containing music for all parts of the service that were to be sung. His music is monodic, and in a plainsong style; some has very clearly been adapted from the Sarum repertory, some would seem to be his own work. The form of notation used suggests that Merbecke was aiming at speech rhythm in performance. The *booke of Common praier noted* passed through no more than a single edition, for the publication of a much revised prayer book in 1552 made the work obsolete. As the preface shows, Merbecke mainly had in mind the needs of parish churches; cathedral music at that time would normally have been on a much more elaborate scale. Although the composer was a lay-clerk and organist at St. George's, Windsor for more than fifty years (*c.* 1530–1585), there is no evidence that he ever wrote part-music for the English rites. Music for comparison: for his Latin compositions see *Tudor Church Music*, Vol. 10 (1929); see also *Cranmer's First Litany, 1544,* and *Merbecke's booke of Common praier noted,* ed., J. E. Hunt, SPCK (1939).

THOMAS TALLIS: **Wherewithal shall a young man cleanse his way?**
                    If ye love me
                    Salvator mundi (With all our hearts and mouths)

The most important Edwardian source of English liturgical music is a small set of choir part-books (known as the Wanley books, from their eighteenth-century owner Humphrey Wanley) now deposited in the Bodleian Library, Oxford (MSS. Mus. sch. e. 420–422). The set originally consisted of four books (AATB), but the tenor book is now unfortunately missing. The greater part of the Wanley music is for men's voices, and probably represents the repertory of a musical city church during the 'experimental' Edwardian years, 1547–1550. Even during those early years the main forms and styles of Anglican music were already current: settings of paired morning and evening canticles, settings of the ordinary of the communion service, and anthems. Tallis wrote music of all these various kinds. *If ye love me* is in the Wanley collection, and it was later published by John Day, in his *Certaine notes*, of 1565.

The daily psalms were normally sung to 'plainsong' chants, harmonised or unharmonised. On festal occasions, however, it became the practice to sing portions of these psalms rather more elaborately. Tallis's three sets of 'festal' psalms are the earliest of their kind; they cover Christmas Day, and the 24th and the 26th evenings of the month. They are unlikely to be earlier than 1552, the date of the publication of the revised *Book of Common Prayer*.

As he grew older Tallis lost none of his zest for life. In 1575, when nearing seventy, he collaborated with a young Chapel Royal colleague of his, William Byrd, to publish a set of Latin 'motets', or as they are described on the title page of the collection, *Cantiones quae ab argumento sacrae vocantur.* Fifteen of the thirty-two compositions are by Tallis. *Salvator mundi,* the first of the two settings of this text, became very popular during the late sixteenth and early seventeenth centuries, both in its original form and in an English adaptation. Tallis died in 1585, having been a Gentleman of the Chapel for forty-five years or more: see 'Thomas Tallis', *Tudor Church Music,* Vol. 6 (1928); see especially *Salve intemerata virgo,* a large-scale votive antiphon; *O nata lux de lumine,* a compline hymn; *In ieiunio et fletu,* an imitative motet in a strikingly original harmonic style; see also *Audivi media nocte,* OUP 1963; *Magnificat* and *Nunc dimittis* from the *Short Service,* OUP 1956; and *Te Deum in five parts,* OUP 1965.

WILLIAM PARSONS: **In trouble and in thrall**

Of the dozen or so Edwardian composers whose names are known, nearly all were members of the Chapel Royal. William Parsons was one of the few exceptions. Shortly before 1550 he became Master of the Choristers at Wells Cathedral and between 1550 and 1560 he was paid various sums by the Dean and Chapter for music that he had composed and copied out for the use of the cathedral choir. Nothing is known of him after 1561, but many of the psalm tunes in Day's *The whole psalmes in foure partes* (*c.* 1563) are harmonized by a William Parsons. For further information see the article in *Grove's Dictionary* (volume V) under 'Psalter'.

ROBERT STONE: **The Lord's Prayer**

Robert Stone, the composer of the popular setting of the Lord's Prayer, joined the Chapel Royal choir sometime between 1547 and 1553. He held this post until his death in 1613 at the venerable age of ninety-seven. No other music of his is known.

WILLIAM MUNDY: **O Lord, the maker of all things**
Ah, helpless wretch

William Mundy became head chorister at Westminster Abbey in 1543. By 1547 he was a layclerk at the city church of St. Mary-at-Hill, and he later moved to St. Paul's Cathedral, probably in about 1550. In 1563 he joined the choir of the Chapel Royal, remaining a member until his death in 1591. He was a prolific composer of devotional and liturgical music, both Latin and English. The text of *O Lord the maker* was first published in the King's Primer of 1545, and reprinted in subsequent Edwardian and Elizabethan Primers.

By 1570, at the latest, composers had begun to make use of solo voices and independent instrumental accompaniments in their anthems. Musicians of the Chapel Royal seem to have led the way, William Mundy, Richard Farrant and Byrd being amongst the earliest composers to use the new 'verse' style. The words of *Ah helpless wretch* were first published by William Hunnis, Master of the Chapel Royal choristers, in a collection of devotional verse and prose entitled *The poore Widowes Mite.* This first appeared in 1583, but its contents may well have been known at Court for some little time before this. Mundy is recorded as having written at least one other verse anthem—*The secret sins*—and there are good reasons for supposing that the work at present attributed to Gibbons is in fact by Mundy; see 'Orlando Gibbons', *Tudor Church Music*, Vol. 4 (1925)—also in 'Orlando Gibbons: Verse anthems', *Early English Church Music*, Vol. 3, Stainer & Bell (1963); for the Latin music see 'William Mundy: Latin Antiphons and Psalms', *Early English Church Music*, Vol. 2, Stainer & Bell (1963).

ROBERT PARSONS: **Nunc dimittis (from the First Service)**

Robert Parsons joined the Chapel Royal choir in 1563. Seven years later he was drowned in the river Trent at Newark. His Service of *4, 5, 6 and 7 parts*, from which this Nunc dimittis comes, closely rivals the late Elizabethan 'Great' Services of Byrd, Weelkes and Tomkins, both in its length and complexity. There are similar settings by other early-Elizabethan musicians, notably William Mundy and Shepherd. Three of Robert Parsons's Services are extant, together with a handful of motets and three anthems: see also 'Deliver me from mine enemies' ed., P. Oboussier, Novello (1954).

THOMAS CAUSTUN: **Nunc dimittis**

But for John Day's *Certaine notes* of 1565 scarcely any of Caustun's music would have survived. Day designed the collection as much for the use of parish churches as cathedrals; the music is simple and in four parts, and much (like Caustun's setting of the Nunc dimittis 'for men') is chant-like in structure. Caustun sang in the Chapel Royal choir from about 1553 until his death in 1569: see also the *Evening Service for Four voices*, by Thomas Caustun, OUP (1963).

RICHARD FARRANT: **Hide not thou thy face**
Lord, for thy tender mercy's sake

Richard Farrant joined the Chapel Royal choir shortly before 1553, but in 1564 he resigned his place in order to become Master of the Choristers at Windsor. Five years later he rejoined the Chapel Royal while continuing to fulfil his duties at Windsor. He died in 1581. Only three anthems of his and a Service are now extant. See also *Evening Service*, by Richard Farrant, OUP (n.d.).

ROBERT WHITE: **Christe, qui lux es et dies**

Robert White was one of the very few early-Elizabethan composers to remain outside the Chapel Royal circle. He took his Mus.B. at Cambridge in 1560 and shortly afterwards he succeeded Tye at Ely Cathedral. He may for a while have been at Chester Cathedral before going to London in 1570 as organist of Westminster Abbey. He died of the plague in 1574. White is chiefly remembered for his Latin music—only three anthems of his have yet come to light—*Lord, who shall dwell, O how glorious art thou* (possibly by Hooper) and *The Lord bless us*. About half of White's Latin compositions are based on non-liturgical psalm-texts, and probably therefore date from 1558 onwards. The liturgical (and therefore Marian) compositions consist of a Magnificat, two antiphons, two sets of Lamentations, a Responsary from the Burial Service—and the Compline hymn, *Christe qui lux es et dies*. The setting published here is one of four; like the others it is in unadorned cantus-firmus style, with small points of imitation ingeniously contrived against the plainsong: see 'Robert White', *Tudor Church Music*, Vol. 5, 1926.

An English translation of the hymn (taken from *Hymns Ancient and Modern*, Historical edition 1909) is here given:

1 O Christ, who art the light and day,
   Thou drivest night and gloom away;
   O Light of light, whose word doth show
   The light of heaven to us below.

4 Asleep though wearied eyes may be,
   Still keep the heart awake to thee;
   Let thy right hand outstretched above
   Guard those who serve the Lord they love.

2 All-holy Lord, in humble prayer,
   We ask tonight thy watchful care;
   O grant us calm repose in thee,
   A quiet night from perils free.

5 Behold, O God our shield, and quell
   The crafts and subtleties of hell;
   Direct thy servants in all good,
   Whom thou hast purchased with thy blood.

3 Our sleep be pure from sinful stain;
   Let not the tempter vantage gain,
   Or our unguarded flesh surprise,
   And make us guilty in thine eyes.

6 O Lord, remember us, who bear
   The burden of the flesh we wear;
   Thou, who dost e'er our souls defend,
   Be with us even to the end.

7 All praise to God the Father be,
   All praise, eternal Son, to thee,
   Whom with the Spirit we adore,
   For ever and for evermore.

WILLIAM BYRD: **Teach me, O Lord**
Nunc dimittis (from the Great Service)
Sing joyfully
Ne irascaris (O Lord, turn thy wrath)
Ave verum corpus
Ave Maria, gratia plena
Kyrie (from the Mass for Four Voices)

William Byrd, one of England's greatest composers, was born in 1543. When only twenty years old he was appointed organist of Lincoln Cathedral, and seven years later he joined the Chapel Royal, resigning his post at Lincoln in 1572. In 1575 he collaborated with his elder colleague Thomas Tallis, to publish a set of *Cantiones quae ab argumento sacrae vocantur*; on the title page of this work he described himself as an organist of the Chapel Royal. He was a prolific composer of devotional and liturgical music, as well as secular solo songs, part-songs, madrigals, and instrumental music. His published works include two sets of *Cantiones Sacrae* (1589 and 1591), three Latin Masses (undated), two books of Latin liturgical compositions, (the *Gradualia* of 1605 and 1607) and three English anthologies of secular and sacred song—the *Psalmes*,

Sonets and songs of sadnes and pietie (1588), the *Songs of sundrie natures* (1589), and the *Psalmes, Songs and Sonnets* (1611).

Although Byrd was at heart a Catholic he wrote a good deal of music for the Anglican rites in all the current forms. The festal psalm, *Teach me, O Lord*, was sung on Epiphany Sunday and is associated in the Durham Cathedral manuscripts with the second set of Preces. It is the earliest known festal psalm in verse-form.

Byrd wrote at least five Services, one in 'Short-Service' style (see Orlando Gibbons, Nunc dimittis, page 185), a five-part Evening Service, an Evening Service 'for verses', a short Morning Service (too incomplete for reconstruction) and a 'Great Service', consisting of Venite, Te Deum, Benedictus, Kyrie, Gloria, Magnificat and Nunc dimittis. This is directly in the tradition of the early Elizabethan 'Great' Services of William Mundy, Robert Parsons and John Shepherd. In some of the pre-Restoration sources sections of the Service are marked 'verse', suggesting that solo voices were occasionally used in performance. The tonality of the setting is notably more 'directional' than that of earlier settings, and there are clear modulations to nearly related 'keys' (compare Robert Parsons, Nunc dimittis, page 33).

On stylistic grounds *Sing joyfully* would seem to be one of Byrd's latest anthems. It may be compared with *O Lord, make thy servant Elizabeth*, OUP (1952) an early work, showing the influence of William Mundy. Byrd wrote comparatively few 'liturgical' anthems; most of those listed in Fellowes's *William Byrd* are devotional part-songs (see Peter le Huray, *English Church Music*, 1540–1640, Herbert Jenkins, Chapter 6).

Ne irascaris was published by Byrd in the 1589 *Cantiones Sacrae*. It was one of his most popular motets, both in its original form and in the English adaptations, of which three different ones exist. *O Lord, turn thy wrath* dates from 1616 at the latest, and may even have been adapted by the composer himself.

Ave Maria and *Ave verum corpus* come from the *Gradualia* of 1605. *Ave Maria* is an Alleluia for performance between the reading of the Epistle and Gospel during Advent; *Ave verum* is a Sequence Hymn for the Feast of Corpus Christi: both were composed for the Roman rites. That Byrd dared and was allowed to publish two such sets of liturgical compositions is in itself extraordinary. That he also published three settings of the mass is even more remarkable. For obvious reasons the printer chose to remain anonymous, and there are no dates on any of the extant copies. That these settings were used at recusant services cannot be doubted. Father William Weston actually met Byrd on one such occasion:

> The following day we left the city and went out nearly thirty miles to the home of a catholic gentleman, a close friend of mine. . . . In the house was a chapel, set aside for the celebration of the church's offices. The gentleman was a skilled musician, and there were an organ, other musical instruments, and choristers, both male and female. During those eight days it was just as if we were celebrating the octave of some great feast . . . Mr. Byrd the very famous musician and organist was among the company. Earlier he had been attached to the Queen's Chapel where he had gained a great reputation. But he had sacrificed everything for his faith . . .
>
> (from *William Weston, The Autobiography of an Elizabethan*, trans. P. Caraman, 1951)

Father Weston was of course mistaken in this, for Byrd was still a member of the Chapel at the time of his death in 1623: see E. H. Fellowes, *William Byrd*, (1948); *The Collected Works of William Byrd*, Stainer & Bell (1937-); 'William Byrd', *Tudor Church Music*, Vol. 2 (1922)—this contains much of the English liturgical music; 'Consort Songs', *Musica Britannica*, Vol. 22 (1965); the Services, and many of the anthems are available separately in the Stainer and Bell edition, and also in the *Tudor Church Music* (octavo) series, published by OUP.

THOMAS MORLEY: **Nolo mortem peccatoris**
                              Out of the deep

In September, 1574, the Dean and Chapter of Norwich granted the young Thomas Morley—then aged about sixteen—the reversion of the office of Organist and Master of the Cathedral Choristers. Payments made to him between 1583 and 1587 show that he was then sharing the duties with an elder colleague. In 1588 he took his B.Mus. at Oxford and at about the same time he left Norwich for London where in the following year he was acting as organist of St. Giles, Cripplegate. By 1591 he was organist of St. Paul's, a post which he quickly resigned after securing a place for himself in the Chapel Royal choir in the following year. During the ten years between 1593 and his death in 1603 he published no fewer than ten sets of madrigals, canzonets, ballets, ayres, and consort lessons, as well as the *Plaine and Easie Introduction to Practicall Musicke*, an extraordinarily comprehensive guide to the theory and practice of music. He is generally regarded as England's first, and one of her foremost madrigalists—see J. Kerman, *The Elizabethan Madrigal*, OUP (1962).

Of his liturgical compositions there now remain a complete Morning, Communion and Evening Service 'for verses', a five-part Evening Service, a 'Short' Evening Service, versicles, responses and a set of festal psalms. *Nolo mortem peccatoris* was probably a devotional song rather than an anthem; the rather unusual range of the inner voice-parts suggests that Morley wrote it for a particular group of singers, and the composite English/Latin text argues against liturgical use. *Out of the deep* was, and still is one of the most popular anthems of its kind. Few other anthems quite equal it in declamatory power. For further study: Thomas Morley, *Collected Motets*, Stainer and Bell, (1959); *Short Evening Service*, OUP (1956); and Thomas Morley, *Magnificat and Nunc dimittis*, OUP (1964).

JOHN BULL: **In the departure of the Lord**

At the age of only twenty John Bull became Organist and Master of the Choristers at Hereford Cathedral through the good offices of Sir Henry Sidney, President of the Council of Wales. Three years later, in January 1586, he was sworn a Gentleman of the Chapel Royal—he had been a chorister there—and by 1591 he was one of the Chapel Royal organists. In 1613 he 'went beyond the seas' without licence and was admitted into the Archduke's service, and entered into pay there [Brussels] about Michaelmas; see, *Cheque Book of the Chapel Royal*, ed. E. F. Rimbault, Camden Society (1872). He

...ed in 1628, having been organist of Antwerp Cathedral for over ten years. Bull was renowned as a keyboard virtuoso, and the greater part of his very considerable output is for organ, harpsichord and virginals. No canticles, psalms or responses of his are known, but there are one or two large-scale anthems and some devotional part-songs, of which *In the departure of the Lord* is a good example; this was published by Sir William Leighton in his *Teares or Lamentacions of a Sorrowfull Soule* in 1614, the year after Bull fled to the Continent. Many of the pieces in this collection are by the leading composers of the day, and many like Bull's *In the departure* are scored for broken consort of treble viol, bass viol, flute, lute, pandora and cittern—see 'John Bull', *Musica Britannica*, Vol. XIV and Vol. XIX, for biographical material and the keyboard music; and *Almighty God, who by the leading of a star*, OUP (1963)—a popular anthem for SSATB soloists, SAATB chorus and viols, or organ.

PETER PHILIPS: **Ascendit Deus**

Peter Philips is said to have been a chorister at St. Paul's Cathedral, and he is mentioned in the will of Sebastian Westcott, Organist and Master of the Choristers there from 1560 to 1582. By 1590 Philips was living abroad, probably in Antwerp or Brussels, and by 1611 he had taken Holy Orders and was organist of the Chapel Royal at Brussels. He died shortly after 1633. He was a prolific composer, publishing no fewer than four sets of madrigals (1591–1603) and a dozen sets of motets for various groupings of voices (1612–1633, and one posthumous publication): Philips's collected motets are in preparation for *Early English Church Music*, Stainer & Bell.

JOHN FARMER: **The Lord's Prayer**

John Farmer preceded Thomas Bateson as organist of Christ Church, Dublin; the earliest record of his appointment there dates from 1595. In 1599 he moved to London where he published a set of four-part madrigals. He does not seem to have written any liturgical music, but he was one of the most important contributors to Thomas East's *Whole Book of Psalms* of 1592 (a successor to John Day's *The whole psalmes*, of 1563). His setting of the Lord's Prayer comes from this collection; the metrical version is the standard one in Sternhold and Hopkins.

THOMAS TOMKINS: **Nunc dimittis (from the Fourth Service)**
Arise, O Lord, into thy resting place

Thomas Tomkins seems to have been the most prolific of all the Elizabethan and Jacobean composers. He wrote an immense quantity of music for stringed and keyboard instruments, thirty or more madrigals and sacred songs and at least seven Services, one-hundred and thirteen anthems, a set of preces, two sets of festal-psalms and several psalm-tunes. He was born at St. David's in Pembrokeshire in about 1572; his father was organist of the cathedral there. In 1596, after spending some time in London (possibly as a pupil of Byrd) he became organist of Worcester Cathedral. No record has survived of his appointment to a place in the Chapel Royal choir; he was witness to a vestry transaction in June 1620, but the odds are that he had been a Gentleman of the Chapel since at least 1612, if not earlier, for in that year he was commissioned to write an anthem for Prince Henry's funeral. In 1621 he succeeded Hooper as an organist of the Chapel, and four years later he provided much of the music for the coronation of Charles I. In 1628 he became 'composer in ordinary' to the king. Nothing is known of his activities at Court after 1628. He retained his post at Worcester until services there were stopped in 1646. For the next six years he continued to live in his house near the cathedral, but in 1654 he moved to his son's house at Martin Hussingtree, where he died two years later.

Of Tomkins's five Services, only the first (a full setting) seems to have been at all well known. The fourth Service, from which this Nunc dimittis is taken, calls for seven soloists (SSAATBB), two independent choirs (each SATB) and an organist of more than average ability.

Arise, O Lord, is one of Tomkins's larger 'full' anthems; it well illustrates the wide range of melodic and harmonic rhythms that the composer often used in his liturgical compositions. Music for comparison: Thomas Weelkes, *O Lord, arise*, (1931); 'Thomas Tomkins', *Tudor Church Music* Vol. 8 (1928), contains the services, preces and psalms; the complete anthems are in preparation for *Early English Church Music*; part 1 is in the press. Many of the anthems are published separately in the Tudor Church Music (octavo) series; *When David heard*, Stainer & Bell (1924) (a sacred madrigal); *My beloved spake*, Schott 10609 (1958); and *O give thanks* (1964)—for men's voices. Several of the anthems for men's voices are also published in *Anthems for Men's Voices, Books I and II*, OUP (1965).

THOMAS WEELKES: **Gloria in excelsis Deo**
Give ear, O Lord

In spite of much recent research nothing is known of Thomas Weelkes before 1597 when he published his first set of madrigals. By 1598 he was organist of Winchester College, and during the next two years he published two further sets of madrigals and ballets. Shortly after taking his B.Mus. at Oxford in 1602 he went to Chichester as Organist and Master of the Choristers, and he remained there until his death in 1623. In 1608 he published his fifth and last work, the *Ayeres or Phantasticke Spirites*, in which he described himself as a Gentleman of his Majesty's Chapel. From 1613, and perhaps even earlier, he went steadily downhill; there are reports in the Chichester archives of drunkenness, negligence and even incompetence. A new choirmaster was appointed in his stead in 1617 though he was allowed to remain there as layclerk and organist, in spite of the bishop's injunctions to the contrary.

Weelkes wrote at least nine Services, of which only three are now complete enough to warrant reconstruction. Of the forty or so extant anthems about half are reasonably complete. In several of the anthems Weelkes experimented in small but unusual ways with various schemes of formal repetition. *Gloria in excelsis* is more or less in ternary form, as is *Alleluia. Give ear, O Lord*, one of the loveliest verse anthems of the period is a kind of rondo, the refrain 'mercy, good Lord, mercy' being varied interestingly at each recapitulation. Repetition forms of this kind are rare in English church music though common on the Continent. See 'The Anthems of Thomas Weelkes', *Musica Britannica*, Vol. 23 (1965)—a complete edition; many anthems are published separately in the Tudor Church Music (octavo) series: see especially *Hosanna to the Son of David* OUP (n.d.); *When David heard that Absalom was slain*, Novello (1956) *Service of Four Parts*, Stainer and Bell (1931); *Magnificat and Nunc Dimittis in Seven parts*, OUP (1965); and *Evening Service for trebles*, Stainer & Bell (1962).

RICHARD DERING: **Factum est silentium**

Richard Dering was born between 1575 and 1585, the natural son of Henry Dering of Liss in Hampshire. In 1610 he supplicated for a B.Mus. at Oxford, 'scholaris in musica exercitatissimus ex aede Christi'. A letter dated June 26th, 1612, from the English ambassador in Venice, Sir John Harrington, mentions a 'Mr. Dearing'. Possibly by 1617 and certainly by 1625 Richard Dering was organist of the Convent of the Benedictine Nuns in Brussels. In 1625 he took up residence in England again, and was a musician 'for the virginals, lutes and voices' to King Charles I. His name appears in Queen Henrietta Maria's establishment book for 1629/30 and it is probable that he was organist of her private chapel in Somerset House. His will was proved on 27th April, 1630. In 1617 and 1618 he published two books of motets, both with basso continuo, and two years later, two books of *Canzonette*. Some small two- and three-part motets appeared in Playford's *Cantica Sacra* of 1662 and 1674. Two verse anthems are all that remain of his music for the anglican rites. *Factum est silentium* was first published in the *Cantica Sacra* of 1618; this highly dramatic setting shows very clearly Italianate 'seconda pratica' influences. Dering's motets are being prepared for publication in *Early English Church Music*, Stainer and Bell.

ORLANDO GIBBONS: **Nunc dimittis (from the Short Service)**
       O Lord, in thy wrath rebuke me not
       See, see, the Word is incarnate

Orlando Gibbons was the youngest of the major Jacobean composers. He was born at Oxford in 1583 and was a chorister at King's College, Cambridge from about 1596 until 1598. He took his Cambridge Mus.B. in 1606, the year after he became a Gentleman of the Chapel Royal. He was considered by many to be the foremost organist of his day; he subsequently became an organist of the Chapel Royal, virginalist to the king, and organist of Westminster Abbey. He died suddenly, probably of an apoplectic fit, while at Canterbury with the Chapel Royal to welcome the new Queen, Henrietta Maria, in 1625.

  Though a prolific composer, he published little—a set of *Madrigals and Motets* in 1612, some pieces for keyboard in *Parthenia* (n.d.) and two sacred songs in Leighton's *Teares* or *Lamentacions* (1614). A great many of his anthems have accompaniments for viols instead of organ (apart from Gibbons's nine anthems there are another thirty or so for voices and viols by various composers, including Amner, Byrd, Bull, East, Edward Gibbons, John Hilton, Hooper, John Mundy, Nicholson, Ravenscroft and Thomas Tomkins). Alternative organ parts exist for many of these anthems. There is little evidence that viols were much used in daily worship, and even at the Chapel Royal they may only have been used on special occasions. *See, see, the Word is incarnate* is one of the most complex and colourful pre-Restoration verse anthems; it is odd to think that the editors of *Tudor Church Music* should have criticized it in the preface to their 1928 edition as being over-elaborate, and even mechanical! *O Lord, in thy wrath* is one of the composer's finest full anthems—it has survived in only one source, Barnard's manuscript collection (Royal College of Music, MSS. 1045-51). The Nunc dimittis from the 'Short' Service was easily the most popular setting of its day, possibly on account of its unusually melodious quality. The underlay of the inner voices, however, is not always as felicitous as could be wished.

For further study: Orlando Gibbons's, *Tudor Church Music*, Vol. 4, (1925); a new edition is in preparation for *Early English Church Music*; part 1 has already appeared (1963) devoted to the verse anthems.

Many separate items are published in the *Tudor Church Music* (octavo) series; see especially, *Hosanna to the Son of David*, OUP (1925); *This is the record of John*, Novello and the *Magnificat and Nunc dimittis*, Novello, (1919).

JOHN AMNER: **Remember not, Lord, our offences**

John Amner was organist and Master of the Choristers at Ely Cathedral from 1610-1641. He was one of the few provincial composers whose music is now of more than historical interest. His extant compositions are all devotional or liturgical—there are two sets of preces, three complete Services, an Evening Service and over forty anthems and part-songs. The present anthem is one of his more ambitious works; the setting of 'amen' in particular is one of the most memorable of the period. See also *A stranger here*, Stainer and Bell (1924); *Love we in one consenting*, OUP (1957); and *O ye little flock*, Church Music Society Reprints (1964).

ADRIAN BATTEN: **O praise the Lord, all ye heathen**

Adrian Batten was a pupil of John Holmes, organist of Winchester cathedral *c.* 1600. In 1614 Batten became a lay-clerk of Westminster Abbey and later a vicar-choral and organist of St. Paul's. Although he lived in London for a considerable time, and although he was a prolific composer, little of his music seems to have been sung by the Chapel Royal choir: only two of the three hundred or more anthems in the Chapel Royal anthem book (*c.* 1635) are by him. His compositions—all for liturgical use—include preces, festal psalms, a litany, a Short Service for men, a Short Service for S.A.T.B., two other full Services, four verse Services and some sixty anthems. His work is never less than competent but rarely inspired. He is at his best in the smaller full and verse forms of which the fourth Evening Service, OUP (1957)—and the third setting of *O praise the Lord* are fair examples. See also: *O praise the Lord*, OUP (1929), and *Out of the deep*, Schott 10573 (1957)—and compare Morley's setting.

WALTER PORTER: **Praise the Lord**

Like his contemporary, John Cooper (alias Coperario), Porter spent some time in Italy where, it seems, he studied with Claudio Monteverdi. By 1616 he was back in England, for in January of that year he was sworn 'for the next place that should fall void by the death of any tenor'. He became a Gentleman of the Chapel exactly a year later, keeping the appointment until the dissolution of the choir in 1642 or 1643. In 1632 he published one Italianate collection of *Madrigales and Ayres*, in which is to be found the verse anthem *Praise the Lord*, all that now survives of his work for the Anglican Church. Words of some ten anthems of his are in the Chapel Royal anthem book of 1635, four full anthems and six verse anthems. If indeed *Praise the Lord* is typical of his church music it is hardly surprising that it was rarely if ever sung outside the Chapel Royal for the solos would have been beyond the reach of all but the most highly skilled singers. In all probability the treble solos were sung by the 'little singing boys' of the King's Private Music—see H. C. de Lafontaine, *The King's Musick* (1909), p. 59 ff; the tenor solos would doubtless have been sung by the composer himself.

WILLIAM CHILD: **O God, wherefore art thou absent from us?**

William Child was also influenced by the Italian composers of the 'seconda pratica', though his music is closer to the English forms and styles than that of his elder contemporary, Walter Porter. He was born at Bristol in 1606 and was a chorister in the cathedral there under the eminent contrapuntist, Elway Bevin. In 1630 he became a lay-clerk of St. George's Chapel, Windsor, and in the following year he took his B.Mus. at Oxford. From 1634 until his death in 1697 he was Master of the Windsor choristers, and soon after the Restoration he became composer for the wind music of Charles II and a Gentleman of the Chapel Royal. He published in 1639 some Italianate settings of metrical psalms 'fitt for private chappells, or other private meetings with a continual base, either for the Organ or Theorbo, newly composed after the Italian way'. His output for the church is prodigious: there are some eighty psalms and anthems and no fewer than seventeen Services, besides separate canticles, festal psalms and the like. Much of his most interesting work seems to date from his early years at Windsor, before the Civil War. This short introit illustrates Child's imaginative grasp of Italianate harmonic progressions and his use of free, recitativo-style rhythms. For a more traditional full anthem see *O Lord God, the heathen* published in Vol. 3 of this series; for a verse anthem with Italianate features see *Turn thou us*, OUP (1964). Several of Child's shorter and comparatively undistinguished full anthems were published towards the end of the last century, of which *O pray for the peace of Jerusalem*, is a fair example, Novello (rev. 1951).

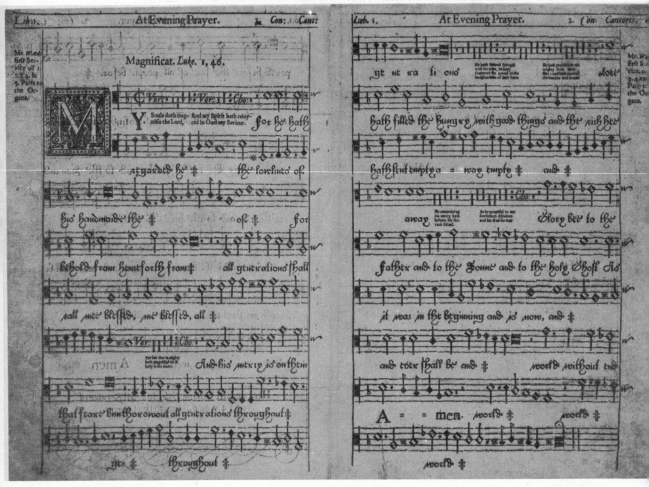

The second alto canton's part of the *Magnificat* from the First Service by John Warde, as printed in Barnard's *First Book of Selected Church Musick*, 1641

(By courtesy of the Dean and Chapter, Lichfield Cathedral)

NUNC DIMITTIS

Transcribed and edited by
JEREMY NOBLE

CHRISTOPHER TYE (c. 1505 - c. 1572)

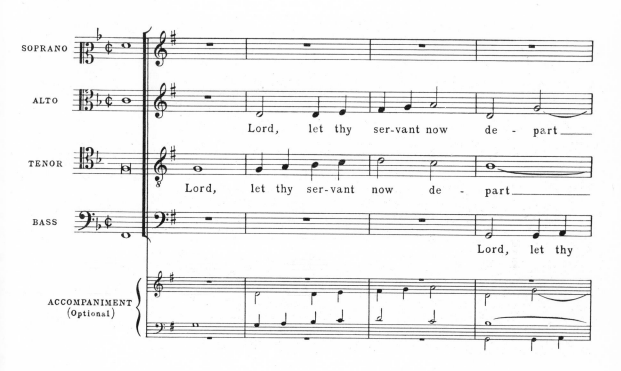

Copyright 1965 by Blandford Press Ltd.

2

NUNC DIMITTIS

Transcribed and edited by
PETER LE HURAY

JOHN MERBECKE (c. 1510-1585)

Lord, now let-test thou thy ser-vant de-part in peace ac-cord-ing to thy word.

For mine eyes have seen, thy sal - va - ti-on, Which thou hast pre-par - ed,

be-fore the face of all peo - ple; To be a light to light-en the Gen - tiles,

and to be the glo-ry of thy peo-ple Is - ra-el. Glo - ry be to the

Fa-ther and to the Son, and to the Ho - ly Ghost; As it was in

the be-gin-ning, is now and e - ver shall be, world with-out end. A - men.

Book of Common Prayer (1549) ## AT THE COMMUNION

The night is pass - ed, and the day is at hand, let us there-fore cast a-

-way the deeds of dark-ness, and put on the ar - mour of light.

AGNUS DEI

O Lamb of God, that tak'st a-way the sins of the world, have mer-cy up-on us.

O Lamb of God, that tak'st a-way the sins of the world, have mer-cy up-on us.

O Lamb of God, that tak'st a - way the sins of the world, grant us thy peace.

Copyright 1965 by Blandford Press Ltd.

WHEREWITHAL SHALL A YOUNG MAN CLEANSE HIS WAY?

FESTAL PSALM

Transcribed and edited by
PETER LE HURAY

THOMAS TALLIS (c. 1505-1585)

Psalm 119: 9-16, for the 24th Day of the Month at Evening Prayer

Where-with-al shall a young man cleanse his way?

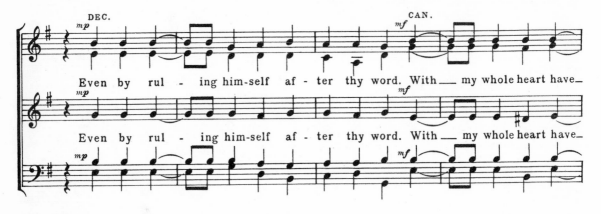

Even by rul-ing him-self af-ter thy word. With __ my whole heart have __

__ I sought thee, O let me not go wrong out of thy com-mand-

ments. Thy words have I hid with-in my heart, that I should not sin a-

*original note values for the intonation

Copyright 1965 by Blandford Press Ltd.

-gainst thee. Bles - sed art thou, O Lord, O___ teach me thy___ sta-tutes.

-gainst thee. Bles - sed art thou, O Lord, O___ teach me thy___ sta-tutes.

With my lips have I been tel - ling of all the judge-ments of thy

With my lips have I been tel - ling of all the judge-ments of thy

mouth. I have had as great de-light in the way of thy tes - ti -

mouth. I have had as great de-light in the way of thy tes - ti -

-mo-nies, as in all man-ner of rich - es. I will talk of thy com -

-mo-nies, as in all man-ner of rich - es. I will talk of thy com -

IF YE LOVE ME

Transcribed and edited by
PETER LE HURAY

THOMAS TALLIS (c.1505–1585)

St. John 14: 15-17

1st ALTO
2nd ALTO
TENOR
BASS
ACCOMPANIMENT (Optional)

If ye love me,—— keep my com-mand-ments,

and I will pray the Fa - - ther, and he shall

Copyright **1965** by Blandford Press Ltd.

SALVATOR MUNDI

(WITH ALL OUR HEARTS AND MOUTHS)

Transcribed and edited by
PETER LE HURAY

THOMAS TALLIS (c.1505-1585)

*The dynamic markings are designed for use with the Latin text. Where the music of the English and Latin versions differs, notes to be used with the English text are shown in small type, with upward stems.

Copyright **1965** by Blandford Press Ltd.

IN TROUBLE AND IN THRALL

Transcribed and edited by
PETER LE HURAY

W. P[ARSONS] (*c.* 1515 after-1561)

Psalm 120, 1-2: Sternhold and Hopkins, 'The whole psalmes in foure parts' (1563)

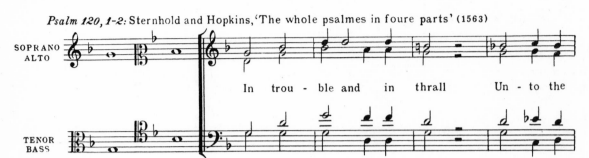

SOPRANO
ALTO

In trou - ble and in thrall Un - to the

TENOR
BASS

Lord I call, And he doth me com -

-fort. De - liv - er me, I say, From li - ers lips

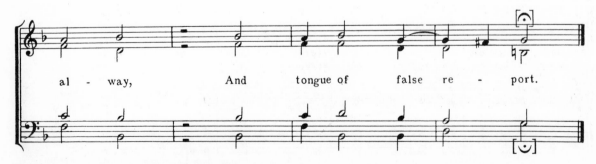

al - way, And tongue of false re - port.

Copyright **1965** by Blandford Press Ltd.

THE LORD'S PRAYER

Transcribed and edited by
PETER LE HURAY

ROBERT STONE (1516-1613)

Copyright 1965 by Blandford Press Ltd.

O LORD, THE MAKER OF ALL THINGS

Transcribed and edited by
PETER LE HURAY

WILLIAM MUNDY (c 1530-1591)

Copyright 1965 by Blandford Press Ltd.

24

AH, HELPLESS WRETCH

Anthem for Alto Solo, Chorus and Organ

WILLIAM HUNNIS (d.1597)
From 'The poore Widowes Mite' (1583)

Transcribed and edited by
PETER LE HURAY

WILLIAM MUNDY (c. 1530-1591)

1. Ah, help-less wretch, what shall I do, or which way shall I go or run?
3. If heav'n and earth shall wit-ness be a-gainst my err-ing soul for sin,

The earth be-wrays the heav'ns re-cord the wick-ed-ness that I have done. Have mer-cy, Lord, for Christ thy Son.
Un-time-ly birth a-las for me a great deal bet-ter had it been than heav'n to loose and hell to win.

Copyright 1965 by Blandford Press Ltd.

S
1st A
mf FULL   20   VERSE

Have mer - cy, Lord, for Christ thy Son.
Than heav'n to loose and hell to win.

2nd A
mf   *p*

Have mer - cy, Lord, for Christ thy Son.
Than heav'n to loose and hell to win.

2. A - las, where shall I
4. Shall I des - pair, thou

T
B
mf

Have mer - cy, Lord, for Christ thy Son.
Than heav'n to loose and hell to win.

mf   *p*

2nd A
25

succ-our find,   both heav'n and earth doth   me de - ny,   So
God for-bid,   I know that mer - cy   more is thine,   Than

30

that un-to the heav'ns a - bove   I dare not once   lift up
if the sins of all the world   were knit and link - - ed un -

35

mine eye,   For I have sinned   so grie-vous-
to mine,   Where - fore my soul   do not re -

NUNC DIMITTIS
FROM THE FIRST SERVICE

Transcribed and edited by
PETER LE HURAY

ROBERT PARSONS (d.1570)

Copyright 1965 by Blandford Press Ltd.

34

Seabury-Western Seminary Library
2122 Sheridan Road
Evanston, Illinois 60201

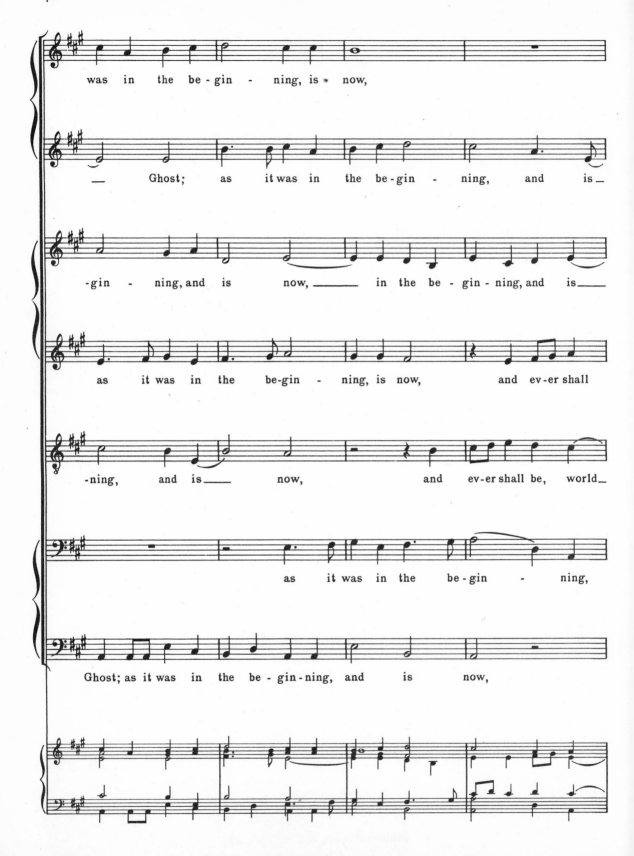

NUNC DIMITTIS

Transcribed and edited by
PETER LE HURAY

THOMAS CAUSTUN (before 1535-1569)

Copyright 1965 by Blandford Press Ltd.

HIDE NOT THOU THY FACE

Transcribed and edited by
PETER LE HURAY

RICHARD FARRANT (before 1535-1581)

Psalm 27: 9

Hide not thou thy face from us, O Lord, and

cast not off thy ser - vants in thy dis - plea - - sure;

for we con - fess our sins un - to____ thee, and hide not our
our un -
our

Copyright 1965 by Blandford Press Ltd.

LORD, FOR THY TENDER MERCY'S SAKE

Transcribed and edited by
PETER LE HURAY

RICHARD FARRANT (before 1535-1581)
also ascribed to JOHN HILTON (the Elder)(before 1565-after 1612)

J. Bull, *Christian Prayers* 1568

Copyright 1965 by Blandford Press Ltd.

CHRISTE, QUI LUX ES ET DIES

Edited by S. TOWNSEND WARNER
Revised edition by
PETER LE HURAY and DAVID WILLCOCKS

ROBERT WHITE (d. 1574)

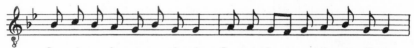

Chri-ste, qui _ lux es et di - es, Noc-tis te-ne-bras de-te-gis

Lu - cis-que lu-men cre-de-ris, Lu-men be - a-tum prae-di-cans.

1st SOPRANO
Pre - ca - mur, sanc - te Do - mi - ne,

2nd SOPRANO
Pre - ca - mur, sanc - te

ALTO
(or TENOR)
Pre - ca - mur, sanc - te

TENOR
(or BARITONE)
Pre - ca - mur, _____ sanc - te

BASS
Pre - ca - mur,

ACCOMPANIMENT
(Optional)

© Copyright 1965 the Oxford University Press, by permission

Ne gra-vis ___ som-nus in - ru - at, Nec hos-tis nos sub-ri-pi-at,

Nec ca-ro il - li con-sen-tiens Nos ti-bi __ re-os sta-tu-at.

O - cu-li som - num

O - cu-li som - num ca - - pi - ant,

O - cu-li som - num ca - -

O - cu - li ____ som - num ca - pi -

O - cu-li som-num ca - pi-ant, ca - -

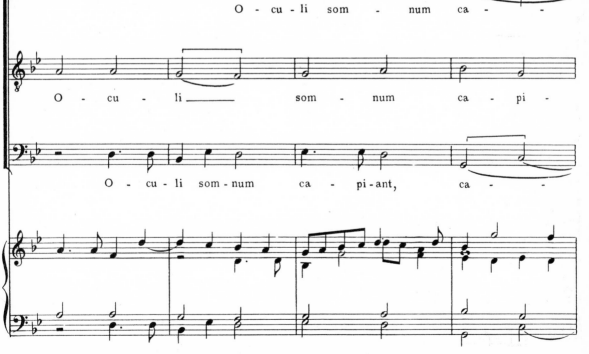

54

For English translation see 'Notes on the music.'

TEACH ME, O LORD

Psalm or Anthem **for Soprano solo, Chorus and Organ**

Transcribed and edited by
PETER LE HURAY

WILLIAM BYRD (1543-1623)

Copyright **1965** by Blandford Press Ltd.

VERSE
(SOPR.)

my whole heart. Make me to go in the path of

__ whole __ heart.

my whole heart.

thy com-mand - ments, for there-in is my de - sire.

In - cline my heart un - to__ thy tes - ti - mon-ies, and__ not to

In - cline my heart un - to__ thy tes - ti - mon-ies, and__ not to

not to co -

and__ not to

* ♩ chord, with pauses in organ

62

NUNC DIMITTIS

FROM THE GREAT SERVICE

Transcribed and edited by
PETER LE HURAY

WILLIAM BYRD (1543-1623)

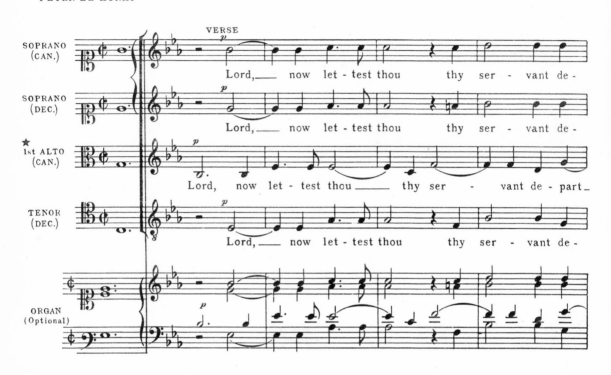

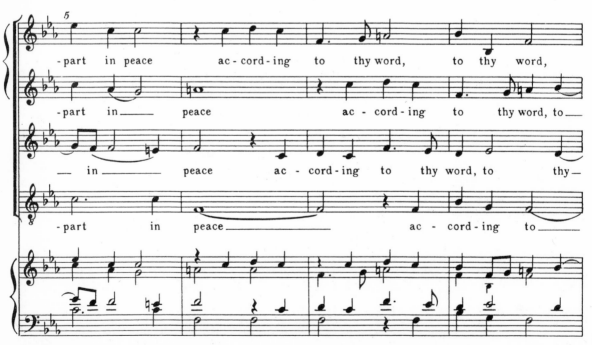

*There are four alto parts: 1st Alto Dec., 1st Alto Can., 2nd Alto Dec. and 2nd Alto Can.

Copyright 1965 by Blandford Press Ltd.

* 2nd Alto Dec. and Can.
** 1st Alto Dec. and Can.

* 2nd Alto Dec. and Can.
** 1st Alto Dec. and Can.

SING JOYFULLY

Transcribed and edited by
PETER LE HURAY

WILLIAM BYRD (1543-1623)

Psalm 81: 1-4

Copyright 1965 by Blandford Press Ltd.

NE IRASCARIS
(O LORD, TURN THY WRATH)

Transcribed and edited by
PETER LE HURAY

WILLIAM BYRD (1543-1623)

*The dynamics are designed for use with the Latin text. Where the music of the English and Latin versions differs, notes to be used with the English text are shown in small type, with upward stems.

Copyright 1965 by Blandford Press Ltd.

AVE VERUM CORPUS

Corpus Christi
Transcribed and edited by
JOHN MOREHEN

WILLIAM BYRD (1543-1643)

Copyright **1965** by Blandford Press Ltd.

ENGLISH TRANSLATION: Hail true Body born of the Virgin Mary: Who
did'st truly suffer, and was sacrificed on
the cross for man's redemption: From whose
pierced side flowed blood: Be to us a source
of consolation at our last hour. O sweet, O
holy, O Jesu Son of Mary, have mercy on me. Amen.

I

AVE MARIA, GRATIA PLENA

Advent
Transcribed and edited by
JOHN MOREHEN

WILLIAM BYRD (1543-1623)

Copyright 1965 by Blandford Press Ltd.

Repeat 1st section only

ENGLISH TRANSLATION: Hail Mary, full of grace,
the Lord be with thee:
blessed be thou among women,
and blessed be the fruit of thy womb. Alleluia.

KYRIE
FROM THE MASS FOR FOUR VOICES

Transcribed and edited by
PETER LE HURAY

WILLIAM BYRD (1543-1623)

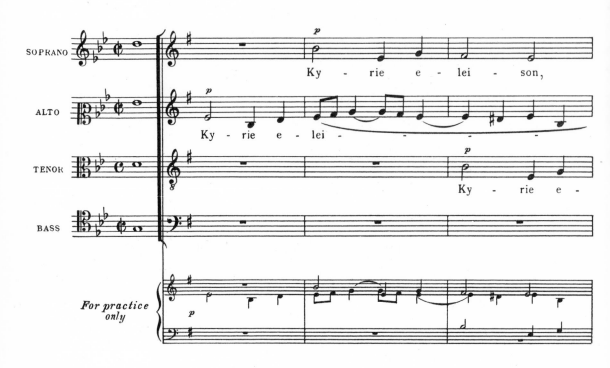

Copyright 1965 by Blandford Press Ltd.

NOLO MORTEM PECCATORIS

Transcribed and edited by
PETER LE HURAY

THOMAS MORLEY (1557-1603)

* English translation : I desire not the death of a sinner : these are the words of the Saviour

Copyright 1965 by Blandford Press Ltd.

20
things ful - fill'd and done ac - cord - ing to thy will, thy will, I
- ther, all things ful - fill'd and done ac - cord - ing to thy will, I
- ther, all things ful - fill'd and done ac - cord - ing to thy will, I
- ther, all things ful - fill'd and done ac - cord - ing to thy will, I
mp
p
25
have. Fa - ther, my will now all is this, No - lo mor - tem pec - ca - to -
have. Fa - ther, my will now all is this, No - lo mor - tem pec - ca - to -
have. Fa - ther, my will now all is this, No - lo mor - tem pec - ca - to -
have. Fa - ther, my will now all is this, No - lo mor - tem pec - ca - to -

OUT OF THE DEEP

Anthem for Alto solo, Chorus and Organ

Transcribed and edited by
PETER LE HURAY

THOMAS MORLEY (1557-1603)

Copyright 1965 by Blandford Press Ltd.

IN THE DEPARTURE OF THE LORD

SIR WILLIAM LEIGHTON (*d.* before 1617)

Transcribed and edited by
PETER LE HURAY

JOHN BULL (*c.*1563-1628)

Copyright 1965 by Blandford Press Ltd.

122

ASCENDIT DEUS

Transcribed and edited by
PETER LE HURAY

PETER PHILIPS (c.1565 - c.1635)

Psalm 47:5

Copyright 1965 by Blandford Press Ltd.

ENGLISH TRANSLATION :   God has ascended with jubilation, and the
Lord with the sound of the trumpet. Alleluia. The Lord
has prepared his seat in Heaven. Alleluia.

THE LORD'S PRAYER

Transcribed and edited by
C. F. SIMKINS
STERNHOLD and HOPKINS

JOHN FARMER (before 1575-?)

Our Fa-ther which in hea - ven art, Lord, hal-lowed be thy name. Thy king-dom come,___ thy___ will be done in earth, ev'n as the same in hea-ven is. Give us, (O Lord,)our dai-ly bread this day, As we for-give our deb-tors, so for-give our debts we pray. In-to___ temp-ta-tion lead us not. From e-vil make us free. For king-dom, power, and glo-ry___ thine, both now and e-ver be.

Copyright 1965 by Blandford Press Ltd.

NUNC DIMITTIS
FROM THE FOURTH SERVICE

Transcribed and edited by
JOHN MOREHEN

THOMAS TOMKINS (1572-1656)

Copyright 1965 by Blandford Press Ltd.

*Consecutives of this nature are not uncommon in Tomkins' organ scores. In this
instance they are furnished by Tenbury MS. 791

ARISE, O LORD, INTO THY RESTING PLACE

Transcribed and edited by
PETER LE HURAY

THOMAS TOMKINS (1572-1656)

Ps. 132: 8-10

Copyright **1965** by Blandford Press Ltd.

clo - thed with right - e - ous - ness,

-ness, with right - - eous -

-ness, with right - eous - ness, with right - e - ous -

be cloth'd with right - e - ous - ness, with right - eous -

priests be clo - thed, be cloth'd with right - eous -

and thy saints sing with joy - ful - ness, with joy - ful - ness,

-ness, and thy saints sing with joy - ful-ness, and

-ness, and thy saints to sing with joy - ful-ness, and

-ness, and thy saints sing with joy - ful - ness, with joy - ful - ness, and

-ness, and

M

GLORIA IN EXCELSIS DEO

THOMAS WEELKES (c.1575-1623)

© Copyright 1965 The Royal Musical Association,
by permission of the Editorial Committee of *Musica Britannica*, (Stainer and Bell)

158

GIVE EAR, O LORD

Anthem for S.S.A.A.T.B. soli, Chorus and Organ

WILLIAM HUNNIS (d.1597)

From 'An humble sute of a repentant sinner for mercie' (1583)

THOMAS WEELKES (c.1575-1623)

© Copyright 1965 The Royal Musical Association, by permission of the Editorial Committee of *Musica Britannica*, (Stainer and Bell)

FACTUM EST SILENTIUM

Transcribed and edited by
PETER LE HURAY

RICHARD DERING (c.1580-1630)

Copyright **1965** by Blandford Press Ltd.

o

ENGLISH TRANSLATION: There was silence in heaven, while the dragon joined battle with the Archangel Michael. A voice was heard – thousands of thousands saying: Salvation, honour and power to Almighty God. Alleluia.

NUNC DIMITTIS
FROM THE SHORT SERVICE

Transcribed and edited by
PETER LE HURAY

ORLANDO GIBBONS (1583-1625)

Copyright 1965 by Blandford Press Ltd.

O LORD, IN THY WRATH REBUKE ME NOT

Transcribed and edited by
PETER LE HURAY

ORLANDO GIBBONS (1583-1625)

Copyright **1965** by Blandford Press Ltd.

194

SEE, SEE, THE WORD IS INCARNATE

Anthem for S.A.A.T.T.B. soli, Chorus and Strings (or Organ)

Transcribed and edited by
JOHN MOREHEN

ORLANDO GIBBONS (1583-1625)

Copyright 1965 by Blandford Press Ltd.

by the preach-ing of glad tid - ings, by the preach-ing of glad

preach-ing of glad tid - ings, by the preach-ing of glad tid - ings

tid - ings of sal-va-ti - on. The blind have

of sal-va-ti - on, glad tid-ings of sal-va-ti - on.

The

VARIANT READING OF BARS 14–17 (as found in B.M. Add.MSS. 29372-6 and Ch. Ch. 56, 57, 59, 60.)

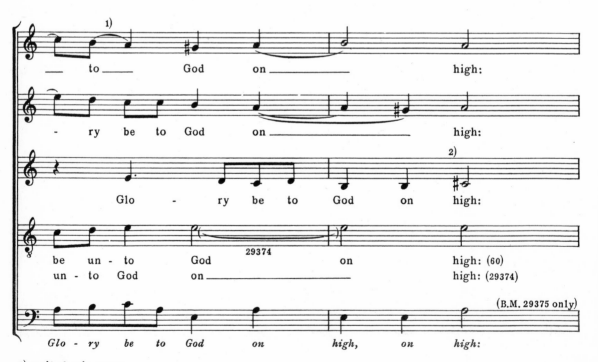

1) omit slur in 29372
2) omit ♯ in 29373

VARIANT ENDING (sources as opposite)

REMEMBER NOT, LORD, OUR OFFENCES

Transcribed and edited by
PETER LE HURAY

JOHN AMNER (c. 1585-1641)

from the Litany

Copyright **1965** by Blandford Press Ltd.

O PRAISE THE LORD, ALL YE HEATHEN

Transcribed and edited by
PETER LE HURAY

ADRIAN BATTEN (before 1590 - c. 1637)

Copyright **1965** by Blandford Press Ltd.

PRAISE THE LORD

Anthem for S.A.T.B. soli, Chorus and Organ

Transcribed and edited by
PETER LE HURAY

WALTER PORTER (*c*.1595-1659)

Copyright **1965** by Blandford Press Ltd.

-fil, ful - fil his com-man - d - ments, com-man - d - ments and

-fil, ye that ful - fil his com-man - d-ments,

ye that ful - fil, ye that ful - fil his com-man - d-ments,

-fil his com - man - d - ments,

heark - en un-to the voice of _____ his word, and

and

un - to the voice of _____ his word, and

and

O GOD, WHEREFORE ART THOU ABSENT FROM US?

Transcribed and edited by
PETER LE HURAY

WILLIAM CHILD (1606-1697)

Copyright **1965** by Blandford Press Ltd.

LIST OF SOURCES

The numbering used is that of the *Catalogue of English Sacred Music, 1549-1644*, by R. T. Daniel and P. G. le Huray, *Early English Church Music* (1966).

PRINTED MUSIC

II AMNER, JOHN, *Sacred Hymns*, 1615.

III BARNARD, JOHN, *The First Book of Selected Church Musick*, 1641.

XIII DAY, JOHN, *Certaine notes set forthe in foure and three partes*, 1565.

XIV DAY, JOHN, *The whole psalmes in foure partes*, 1563(?).

XXII LEIGHTON, SIR WILLIAM, *The Teares or Lamentacions of a Sorrowfull Soule*, 1614.

XXIII MERBECKE, JOHN, *The booke of Common praier noted*, 1550.

XXVI PORTER, WALTER, *Madrigales and Ayres*, 1632.

XXVII TOMKINS, THOMAS, *Musica Deo Sacra*, 1668.

MANUSCRIPTS

I University of California, MS. M2. C645 late 17th century. organ

21-6 Pembroke College, Cambridge, MSS. Mus. 6.1-6. *c.* 1640. MD.CtD, TD, TC, BD, BC

27-33 *Peterhouse, Cambridge, the first 'Caroline' set of part-books, *c.*1635. MD. MC, CtD 1 and 2, CtC, BD, BC

34-40 *Peterhouse, Cambridge, the second 'Caroline' set of part-books, *c.*1635. MD, MC, CtD, TD, TC, BD, BC

47-82 Durham Cathedral Library

47	MS. A1	*c.*1635	O
48	A2	*c.*1635	O
49	A3	*c.*1635	O
51	A5	*c.*1635	O
53	C1	*c.*1635	M
57	C4	*c.*1635	2CtD
58	C5	*c.*1635	2CtC
59	C6	*c.*1635	1CtD
60	C7	*c.*1635	1CtC
62	C9	*c.*1635	TD
63	C10	*c.*1625	TC
64	C11	*c.*1660	TD
65	C12	*c.*1675	TD

*See Dom A. Hughes, *Catalogue of the Musical Manuscripts at Peterhouse Cambridge*, Cambridge, 1953.

66	C13	c.1660	T
68	C15	c.1625	TD
69	C16	c.1660	B
70	C17	c.1675	BD
72	C19	c.1675	B
74–81	E4–11	c.1630	MD, MC 1 CtC 2 CtD & C TD, TC BC
82	MS. E11a	c.1625	Ct
87	Ely Cathedral MS. 4	c.1660	O
89	Ely Cathedral MS. 28	c.1660	T
93	Gloucester Cathedral	c.1640	B
95	Gloucester Cathedral	c.1660	TD

116–220 London, British Museum

116	Add. MS. 15166	c.1570	Tr
118–123	Add. MSS. 17786–91		S, M, Ct, T, Sx, B
136–139	Add. MSS. 18936–9	c.1625	C, A, T, B
144	Add. MS. 29289	c.1625	A
148–53	Add. MSS. 29372–7, (The Myriell Part-Books)	1616	C, A, T, B, Q, S
168–72	Add. MSS. 30480–4	c.1585	C, A, T, B, Q
205	Harley MS. 6346	c.1670	Anthem texts
209	Harley MS. 7340 (a Tudway score)	c.1720	Score
220	Roy. Mus. Lib. MS.23.l.4	c.1590	Score
230	Lambeth Palace Library, London	c.1630	B

235–41	Royal College of Music, London	c.1625	MD, MC CtD, CtC TD, TC BC
259–62	New York Public Library, Drexel MSS. 4180–4	c.1625	C, A, T, B, Q, Sx
266	New York Public Library, Drexel MS. 5469	c.1630	O

290–301 Bodleian Library, Oxford

290–4	MSS. Mus.sch.d. 212–6	c.1615	M, Ct, T, B, Q
296–8	MSS. Mus.sch.e. 420–2	c.1548	Ct. 1 and 2, B
301	MS. Rawl. poet. 23	c.1635	Anthem texts

302–66 Christ Church, Oxford

302	MS. 6	c.1630	O
303	MS. 21	c.1660	Score
306	MS. 47	c.1680	O
307–311	MSS. 56–60	c.1620	C, Q, Ct, T, Sx
319	MS. 88	c.1660	O
321	MS. 437	c.1675	O
354	MS. 1001	c.1640	O
362–6	MSS. 1220–4	c.1640	AD, TD, TC, BD, BC

391–413 St. Michael's College, Tenbury

391	MS. 791	c.1630	O
392–6	MSS. 807–811		M, 1Ct., 2Ct., T, B
412	MS. 1382	c.1617	T
413	MS. 1442	c.1670	B
445	York Minster Library, MS. M.18(S)	1618	MD
446	York Minster Library, MS. M.29(S)	c.1640	B

EDITORIAL METHOD

PREFATORY STAVES   Prefatory staves show the original clefs, first sounding notes, time- and key signatures.

BARRING   Bar-lines are editorial unless otherwise stated in the Textual Commentary.

TRANSPOSITION   The music has been transposed, where necessary, to suit modern conditions of performance.

EDITORIAL ADDITIONS   Small notes, words in square brackets, dynamics and names of parts are editorial. Accidentals in square brackets are to be found in some, but not all sources. Accidentals in round brackets are monitary.

EDITORIAL CORRECTIONS   These are listed in the Textual Commentary below. The system of reference used is best illustrated by an example: 7.iv.2: A (172) implies that in the seventh bar, the fourth voice-part (counting downwards), the second note in the bar, the original would have been A in the modern edition, using source 172 (see above for List of Sources). Rests are counted as notes for purposes of reference: e.g. in a bar containing crotchet, crotchet rest, crotchet, the second crotchet would be numbered 3. A note tied from a previous bar is numbered 0. The following abbreviations are used in the Commentary:
b: breve; s: semibreve; m: minim; c: crotchet; q: quaver; sq: semiquaver; $c.$: dotted crotchet, etc. Pitch is indicated by the use of capital letters. Organ parts are referred to by the use of rh. and lh., and where necessary up. and low.: e.g. 7.rh.up.2: indicates bar 7, right hand, the upper line, and the second symbol.

UNDERLAY   Variants in underlay are innumerable, and seem to be the result as often as not of indifference, as of any specific intention. Only major variants have accordingly been listed in the Commentary.

ORGAN PARTS   These have been supplied from original sources as far as possible. No organ parts exist, however, for the Latin compositions, or for a number of the anthems, and editorial keyboard reductions of the voice-parts have accordingly been supplied. The absence of a prefatory stave against such a part indicates the lack of an original. No attempt has been made to iron out minor discrepancies between the extant organ- and voice-parts, since these are often of some musical and historical interest.

TEXTUAL COMMENTARY

CHRISTOPHER TYE: **Nunc dimittis**

Sources: 168–71 and 296–8.

Variants: This piece anon. in 296–8 / 7.iv.2: A (171) / 8.ii and 9.iii: bracketed words only in 169–170 / 19.iii.1–20.iii.4: *m.BcBc.AqGqF♯qEqGqF♯* (170) / 31.i.2: ♯, 297 only / 32.ii.3: ♯, 296 only / 33: dotted barline represents sectional barline in all sources / 37.ii.1–2: *mm* (169) / 46.ii.2: be *c* to *q* the *q* (169) / 51.ii.1–3: *cGqF♯qE*, only (both sources) / 52.ii.4: *m* (169) / 57.i.3: ♯, 297 only / 59.iv.1–2: *m* (171) / 62.iii.2: ♯ inserted by analogy with 63.i.2 (this voice lacking in 296–8) / 63.i.2: ♯, 297 only / 67: be *m* it *m*, all parts (168–71) / 69–end: all parts have 'Amen' (168–71) / 71.iv.1–end: *b* only (171).

JOHN MERBECKE: **Nunc dimittis, Communion Anthem and Agnus Dei**

Source: XXIII.

Merbecke explains in the preface the meaning of the four kinds of note shape to be found in the book. The 'strene' note is worth a breve, ▪ , the 'square' a semibreve, ▪ , and the 'pycke' a minim ◆ , while the 'close' marks the end of a piece ▪ . Although Merbecke may not have intended that these values should be interpreted with mathematical exactness, he certainly intended that the natural word rhythms and stresses should be brought out in the music. Solesmes-style performances of Merbecke are quite unhistorical, therefore.

THOMAS TALLIS: **Wherewithal shall a young man cleanse his way? (Festal psalm).**

Source: III, also 95, 230, 235–41, 362–6, 435 and 446.

Variants: 12.iii.1: missing (III). The daily psalms were normally sung to plainsong intonations; on special occasions, however, harmonized settings were used. Three sets of festal psalms by Tallis have survived; the second set comprises the proper psalms for Christmas Day, and the other two the appointed psalms for the 24th and 26th evenings of the month. It seems likely therefore that Tallis wrote the three sets for Christmas Eve, Christmas Day and for evensong on the following day.

THOMAS TALLIS: **If ye love me**

Sources: XIII, 49, and 296-8; also 64, 70, 72, 116, 144, 166-7, 259-62 and 302.

The earliest version of the anthem (296-8) is rather simpler than the one published by Day (XIII).

Variants: 4.i.1: *c.q*(296) / 4.ii.1: *c.q*(297) / 6.i.3-7.i.1: *m*G only (296) / 9.iv.2: *c* and *c*-rest (298).

THOMAS TALLIS: **Salvator mundi (With all our hearts and mouths)**

Sources: Tallis and Byrd, *Cantiones quae ab argumento sacrae vocantur* (1575) (Latin version), III (English version) and 1 (organ reduction—English version only).

The musical texts of the Latin and English versions are by no means identical, as may be seen from this conflation.

WILLIAM PARSONS: **In trouble and in thrall**

Source: XIV.

Metrical translations of the psalms first began to appear in England during the reign of Edward VI. From 1559 onwards these achieved enormous popularity both in the church and in the home. Day's edition of *The whole psalmes in foure parts* was the first harmonized edition of the complete Sternhold and Hopkins psalter to be published.

ROBERT STONE: **The Lord's Prayer**

Sources: XIII and 296-8.

The setting in both sources is for men's voices. It should be sung flexibly, the note values being regarded as indications of stress rather than of exact duration.

Variants: k.s. in ii and iv missing (XIII) / 1- hal*c*low*q*ed*c*(296-8) / 2: low bass F also (296-8) / 3: F♯(296-8) / 4: temp*c*tac.ti*q*on*m*(296-8) / 5: no E♭ (296-8) / The final phrase, beginning 'but deliver us . . .' is repeated in 296-8 / 6: F♯ XIII / 7: evil F*m*AG*m*A*c*F*c* men G♭ / The pause marks are inconsistently placed in XIII.

WILLIAM MUNDY: **O Lord, the maker of all things**

Sources: III, 49, 144, 259-62, 362, 364-6; also 266, 302, 319 and 354.

Variants: 4.ii.3: ♭(259) / 2.r.h.1-2: A♭(49) / 5.ii.4: A♭(259) / 6.ii.2-7.ii.1: *cm*(261) / 7.i.1: *cc*(260) / 7.i.2: ♭(260) / 7.ii.2: *c.q*B♭ (259) / 9.ii.3: through *q* thy *q*(261) / 10.ii.3: ♭(144, 259), and also 11.ii.3 / 14.ii.1: ♭(250) / 16.i.3: C(III) / 16-24: the antiphonal arrangement of dec. and can. is unique to III / 19: with dream nor fantasy (259-62) / 22.i.3: *m*(III) / 23.ii.1-2: *c.q*(259) / 29.i.3: *m*. (no *c*-rest) (260) / 33.ii.1-34.ii.1: *cccm*(259) / 38.ii.1: ♭(259) / 42.i.2-end: missing in 259-62; this fifth part is not essential to the harmony, and may well be a seventeenth-century addition. There are no repeat marks in 144, or 259-62; the repeat is fully written out in 49, with minor (unrecorded) variations. / 45.iii.1-46.ii.2: *mmc*.D*q*E♭ (259 / 46.v.2: ♭(262).

WILLIAM MUNDY: **Ah, helpless wretch**

Sources: III (second alto missing, except in the last chorus), 57–60, 62–3, 93, 166, 236, 238, 241, 391.

Variants: the chorus clefs are the normal alto, tenor and bass; the treble is ′C′4. The first and second alto parts in the choruses are reversed. 19.v.1–2: *m*A♭, no *c*-rest (241) / 37–44. The tonality of this chorus is unclear since the sources contain so many conflicting accidentals / 38.l.h.3: ♭(391) / 40.iv.5: *qq*, not *c*(III) / 42.iv.1: *cc*, not *m*(III) / 45.time sig. C3: note values have been halved / 62–end: in (III) the first also is A1 dec., and can.; the second alto is A2, dec., and can. / 64.v.1: *cc*(III).

ROBERT PARSONS: **Nunc dimittis (from the First Service)**

Sources: III, 74–81, and 445.

Variants: 6.iv.3–4: *cc*(III can.) / 6.v.3–4: *c.q*(III dec.) / 11.i.3: *s* all sources / 15.i.1: of *c* all *c* thy *qc*(74) / 18.iv.4: B(all sources except 77) / 20.v.3: A(78) / 22.iv.4: C♯ III dec.) / 24.ii.2: C♯(III dec.) / 25.iv.3: F♯*m*F♯*c*(75–6) / 29.vii.3–4: *c.q*(III) / 39.iii.3: E(III) / 39.vii.2: *m* only (III) / 40.vii.1: Ho*c*ly *c* Ghost *m* as *c*. it *q*(III) / 44.v.2: G♯(III dec.) / 45.iii.2: C♯(III) / 48.i.2–3: *q*E only (III) / 49.vii.i: C♯ (78) / 52.iii.4: G♯(III) / 54.i.2: B(79) / 54.iii.2–3: omitted(III) / 56.v.2: *bb*(77,81) / 58.iii.1–3: A*c*.B*q*(III).

THOMAS CAUSTUN: **Nunc dimittis**

Source: III.

The music should be sung in free rhythm, the note values being primarily an indication of stress. The bar-lines are original; there are however some small discrepancies between the four part books, viz. 1: no bar-line in AI / 2: no bar-line in T / 3: no bar-line in T / 4: crochet only / 5: no bar-lines in AI, T or B.

RICHARD FARRANT: **Hide not thou thy face**

Sources: III, 144, 354v, 362–6; and a number of late seventeenth-century manuscripts.

It is remarkable that the earliest source of this little anthem dates from as late as 1640. 18.rh.3–20.rh.1: F and D♭ *c*, D♭ and B♭ *m*, C and A♭ *m* (354v).

RICHARD FARRANT: **Lord, for thy tender mercy's sake**

Sources: 209, 321 and 362–6; also 87 and 89.

There are no pre-Restoration sources of this anthem. It is attributed to 'Farrant' in 362–6 (*c.* 1670), it is anonymous in 87, 89 and 321, and only in the rather unreliable 209 (*c.* 1720) is it attributed to Hilton. The anthem is in the early Elizabethan bar-form plan, ABB; it could equally well be the work of Richard Farrant, (d. 1581), John Farrant I or II, or John Hilton the elder (d. 1608).

Variants: 9: both 'life' and 'lives' in 362–6 / 9.ii.1: D(209) / 14 l.h. up: *m*A*c*B(321) / 16.i.2: D(209) / 18.iii.1: B(209) / 18.iv.5: C(209) / 19.iii.2: B(209) / 19.iv.2: lower G(366) / 20.ii.4: *q*D*q*C(209). There is a concluding Amen in the Ely sources, which is incomplete, and possibly spurious.

ROBERT WHITE: **Christe, qui lux es et dies**

(see notes in OUP edition)

Sources: III, 74–81, 82 and 302.

The chorus clefs are the normal alto, tenor and bass. The distribution of the alto parts in (III) is as follows: A1: first and second contratenor dec., A2: first and second contratenor can.

Variants: 20.i.3–4: *cc*(79) / 22.i.2: ♮(79) / 26.i.3: *cccCcC*(74) / 28.v.1: low A♭ *m*, not D♭ (III) / 29.ii.2–30.ii.3: *c*A♭,*q*B♭,*m*C,*m*C(75) / 38–45: source 74–81 differs substantially from (III)—see below / 39.i.1–2: *c*A♭ only (79) / 41.i.2: C(74) / 47.i.1–2: *c*-rest*c.q*(79) / 50.i.5–51.i.4: *m*D♭,*m*B♭(79) / 52.org.1: *c*-rest(302) / 53.org.4: *m.*(302) / see below for the final chorus, as given in 74–81.

alternative version of bars 38-45, on page 62

alternative version of the final chorus on page 63

WILLIAM BYRD: **Nunc dimittis (from the Great Service)**

Sources: 21–6, 27–33, 35–6, 48, 74–81 and 82.

The service is scored for two antiphonal five-part choirs (each SAATB). The organ doubles the voices throughout, and may be dispensed with, if preferred. The clefs of the chorus sections are the normal ones.

Variants: 2.ii.2: ♮(79) / 13.v.1: –va*ctiqm*(25–6) / 15.i.1: –va*c.tiqm*(21) / 17.v.1: va*c.tiqmonm. salc*(25–6) / 50.v̈.1: I*sc.raqqqcelc*, peo*qpleq*(25) / 51.ii.4: *cqq*(21) / 54.vi.2: –ra*qqmel*(26) / 54.vi.2: –ra*qqmelm*(26) / 56.ii.1: *m*, not *cc*(21) / 58.v.3: *c.q*(24) / 66.v.1–2: *c.q*(30) / 81.ii.2: and *c* ever *c* shall *c* be *m*(76) / 90.iv.1: missing (81) / 102.iv.2: missing (24).

WILLIAM BYRD: **Sing joyfully**

Sources: 148–53 and 47; also III, 21–6, and 290–4.

Source 290–4 contains a version to be found in no other pre- or post-Restoration source. It contains two major variants: a) the entries in bars 1–3, entry one beginning BB etc, entry two (S1) G♯, G♯, and entry three (A1) EE: at the words 'blow the trumpet in the new moon' there is considerably more cross rhythm—the alternative passage is printed in full below. Possibly this represents an earlier version of the anthem; if so, it is interesting to note that Byrd simplified the rhythms on revision, at the same time brightening the texture by raising the pitch of the upper voices.

Variants: 6.r.h.low.2: F♯(47) / 10.r.h.up.3–11.r.h.up.1: also *m*E,*m*A(47) / 13.ii.4–5: *c* tied to following *q* (290) / 20.ii.1: C♯(148) / 27.v.3–4: *c.q*(293) / 38.v.1–2: *cc*.(293) / 40.ii.4–5: *qq*(290) / 58.i.2–4: *cq*(294) / 62.ii.3–4: *cq*(290).

The A2 is lacking

WILLIAM BYRD: **Ne irascaris (O Lord, turn thy wrath)**

Sources: Byrd, *Cantiones Sacrae*, 1589 (Latin), III (English adaptation), and I (organ).

The underlay of the English version in III is not always clear; the English text in the present edition follows Barnard as closely as possible.

Variants: 2.l.h.up.3: F♯(I) / 36.iv.1: no (III) / 46.r.h.low: the inner part starts at the beginning of the bar, one beat too early (I) / 55.r.h.2–57.r.h.O: an octave higher (I) / 57.r.h.1–58.r.h.3: a third too high (I).

WILLIAM BYRD: **Ave verum corpus**

Source: Byrd, *Gradualia*, 1610 (second edition, Christ Church Oxford) 1605 (first edition, York Minster).

41.iii.3: mi*c*.se*q*re*c*q*req*, the first time.

WILLIAM BYRD: **Ave Maria, gratia plena**

Source: Byrd, *Gradualia*, 1605 (first edition, York Minster).
                              1610 (second edition, Christ Church, Oxford).

WILLIAM BYRD: **Kyrie** (from the Mass for Four Voices)

Source: Byrd, *Mass for Four Voices*, n.d. (*c.* 1600).

The underlay was not printed in full, repeat signs being used in many places. The modern text has been italicized wherever ambiguities arise in the original through use of these signs.

THOMAS MORLEY: **Nolo mortem peccatoris**

Source: 148–51.

The use of a mezzo-soprano clef for the upper part (see prefatory staves) suggests that the part may originally have been intended for a low mean or treble voice. The piece may equally well be transposed upwards a minor third for SAABaritone, or downwards tone for ATTB. The rather unusual tessitura of the inner parts (both have roughly the same range) suggests that Morley may well have had a particular group of singers in mind when he wrote the song.

THOMAS MORLEY: **Out of the deep**

Sources: III, 236, 238, 240, 362–6, 391 and 412; also 34–40, 51, 53, 57–60, 62–64v, 69, 72, 166–7, 230, 266, 306, 319, 413, 446, and a number of post-Restoration sources. The clefs of the chorus parts are the usual ones (S='C' 5, key sig B♭). The alto parts in (iii) are arranged as follows: solo; contratenor dec., and can., i; chorus A1: first contratenor dec., and can; A2: second contratenor dec., and can. 15.iv.3: · (iii) / 33.iii.1: ♮ (362) / 34.iii.3: B♭ all sources / 36: 'but there is mercy' (362–6) / 38.iii.3: A (iii, 236) / 52.iv.1–3:m.B♭, cE♭ (iii) / 77.v.1–2: m, not cc (365–6) / 80: first chord semibreve in 362–6 /

T

JOHN BULL: **In the departure of the Lord**

Source: XXII. All the parts are printed together in one book, arranged thus on facing pages:

Bull has supplied parts for three plucked instruments: lute, cittern (a kind of guitar, with metal frets and strings), and bandora (a larger form of cittern)
7.cittern: first chord c only /14.cittern: the third chord consists of four notes, viz. BF♯EB, and the fourth of three, A♯F♯C♯ /20.bandora: c-rest lacking /

PETER PHILIPS: **Ascendit Deus**

Source: Philips, *Cantiones sacrae* (Antwerp, 1612).

The underlay is particularly clear in this source. 29.iii.1: ♯ (sic) / 39.iii.2–42.iii.1: 'alleluia', underlay uncertain, and repeat mark only in the next phrase / 51: time sig. 3/2: note values have been halved /

JOHN FARMER: **The Lord's Prayer**

Source: Thomas East, *The Whole Booke of Psalms* (1592).

THOMAS TOMKINS: **Nunc dimittis (from the Fourth Service)**

Sources: XXVII and 391.

Variants: 1–12 (II and III) additional *m*-rest / 6–7.r.h. no tie (xxvii) / 7.l.h.up.5: ♭(xxvii) / 8.l.h.low.1: ♮(391) / 9.ii.2: D / 16.vi.1: extra *s* and *c* rests bass can. / 16.i and ii: *c*-rest lacking / 19–20.r.h.: no tie (xxvii) / 22.ii.1: E♭ / 24.iii.1: D / 24.i.3: *q* only / 25.v.3: A♭ / 26.v.3–4: *c*G only / 27.v.4: C / 35.l.h.2–3: *q.sq*(xxvii and 391) / 36.v.1: *s*-rest lacking / 38.r.h.low.1–2: *q.sq*(xxvii) / 44.r.h.low.3: ♭(xxvii) / 47.v.3: thy *q* peo*c*ple *c* Iscrae*c.sqsqc.sqsq*me*l*m / 55.r.h.low.1: ♭(391) / 55.r.h.up.2: no ♭(391) / 55.l.h.1–2: *cc.* (xxvii) / 56.r.h.up.2: no ♭ (xxvii) / 60.iii.1: additional *b*- and *m*-rests / 60.v.1: extra *m*-rest / 60.ii.2: as *c*. it *q* was *c* in *c* the *c* be*c*.gin*qqq*ing*cc* and *c* is *m* now *c* / 62.org.: both versions incompatible with voice-parts / 64.r.h.up.3: no ♮(391) / 69.iii.2: world *q* with*c*out *c* end *c* A*c*men *m*, world *m* with*m*out *m* end *c* A*mc*men *m.*

THOMAS TOMKINS: **Arise, O Lord, into Thy resting place**

Source: XXVII. There are several errors, as follows: 7.iv.4: a*q*rise*cc* / 17.iv.3: *c* not *m* / 21*j*ii.5: *q* only / 29.i.6: -ness*q*with*c*joy*q*ful*q.sqq*ness*m* / 32.iii.1: -ful*sq*ness*qc* / 36.iii.6: with*q*joy*q*.ful*sqq*ness*q*.with*sq*joy*q* -/ 36.iv.3–4: *q*.E♭, *sq*D / 40.iv.3: G / 51.1h.up and low.3: *m*. / 60.i.1: G / 64.iii.4: a*sq*noints*qm*.

THOMAS WEELKES: **Gloria in excelsis Deo**

Sources: 118–123 / 307–311 / 392–396 / 412.

Variants: 3.iv.5: o(394) / 4.v.1–19.v.1: 'Gloria in excelsis Deo' appears as 'Glory be unto God the Lord' in 412 / 8.ii.4: o(392) · 10.i.1: in *c* ex*q*cel*qc*.sis *q* De*com*(307) / 11.iii.2: omitted(122) / 21 *et passim*: 'the Lord' (118–123, 307–311), 'the Lord', 'thine Lord', and 'thy Lord' (392–396) / 26.vi.2: *c.q*(396) / 28.ii.4: o(308, 392) / 28.iii.1: all *c* in *c* glo*c*ry's *sq* *c*(393) / 29 *et passim*: 'thine angels' choir' and 'the angels' choir in 307–311 and 392–396 / 30.v.1–2: *c.q*(309, 395) / 32 *passim*: 'aboard' (118–121, 123 and 412) / 33.iii.1: *m* or *m*-rest lacking (122) / 35 *passim*: 'their highest holy day', and 'the highest holy day' in 307–311, 392–396 and 412; 118–123 has 'the highest holy day' / 36.iv.2–3: *m*.(120) / 37.ii.3: *cc*(308, 392) / 39.iv.1: Crave *m* thy *c* God *m* to *c* thy *m*. heart *c*(120) / 40.v.2: God *c* to *c* tune *c* thy heart *m*(121) / 42.i.1: d♭(307) / 42.i.2: ♯(118) / 43.*passim*: 'unto glory's' (120, 123) / 52.iv.3: o(307) / 53.iii.2: C(393) / 53.v.1–71.v.1: omitted(412) / 56.ii.3: o(308) / 57.ii.2: in *c*. ex*c*el*c*sis *c* De*com*(392) / 58.ii.3: o(308, 392) / 65.v.2: D(395) / 70.iii.4: *c*(122) / 74.iv.2: o(311, 394).

THOMAS WEELKES: **Give ear, O Lord**

Sources: 148–152, 391.

Variants: the clefs in the full sections are the normal ones (S is 'C'5). The text comes from William Hunnis' 'An humble sute of a repentant sinner, for mercie' (1583). 28.r.h.2: D(391) / 45.l.h.low.2–46.l.h.low.1: *c*G♯*c*F♯*c*G♯(391) / 69.i.3: *m*, no *c*-rest(150).

RICHARD DERING: **Factum est silentium**

Source: Dering, *Cantica Sacra*, Antwerp, 1618.

A separate (unfigured) instrumental bass is given in the original, and printed in large notes in the keyboard reduction of this edition.

Errata: 23.iv.1: 'dum' begins on the previous *s* / 33.iii.2: F♯ / 39.v.2: missing / 54.v.2: F♯ / 95.vi.1 and lh.low.I: B.

ORLANDO GIBBONS: **Nunc dimittis (from the Short Service)**

Sources: 220 and 354: also III.

Source 220 is the earliest of the extant sources. Its writer, Benjamin Cosyn, scored six Services, of which Gibbons's very popular Short Service is one, describing them as the six Services of the 'King's Chapel'. This rather suggests that he may have had access to Chapel Royal part-books—Gibbons was of course a Gentleman of the Chapel at that time. Unfortunately Cosyn underlaid only the treble part in his score, providing sketchy incipits for the lower voices. 220 has therefore been collated with Barnard's version, in III. The underlay of the inner parts is poor in all sources. Cosyn barred his score regularly, as in the present edition. Italicized underlay is editorial.

Variants: 5.iv.4: D(220) / 11.ii.3: *qq*(III) / 14.ii.1–3: *m* only (III) / 28.iii.3: *cqq*(220) / 29.iii.1–30.iii.3: *ccccc* (220) / 31.iv.1–2: *m*(III) / 32.iv.1: *cc*(III) / 35.i.2: and ever shall be, world without end (III)—the Amen begins 37.i.6 / 36.ii.2: and ever shall be world without end (III), the Amen begins 38.ii.6 / 39–40.ii: the also part does not divide in III or (220).

The service is full throughout in III; the decani and cantoris markings are in (220) only.

ORLANDO GIBBONS: **O Lord, in thy wrath rebuke me not**

Source: 235–41, also 205 and 301.

27 *passim*: the word 'heal' occasionally appears as 'hear'.

ORLANDO GIBBONS: **See, see, the Word is incarnate**

Sources: 148–152, 303, 307, 308, 310, 311.

The modernization of the key-signature has resulted in the addition of F sharps in the following places:

7(i, v) 11(ii) 12(iv) 13(iii) 14(v, vi) 18(iii) 19(iv) 21(v) 27(iii) 31(i, v) 32(i) 33(v) 34(ii, v) 35(ii, iv) 36(v) 37(ii) 38(i, v) 40(ii) 41(v) 42(ii) 43(ii, iii) 44(i, ii, v) 48(ii) 49(ii, iii) 50(v) 51(iii, v) 52(iii) 53(ii) 55(i, iv) 56(i) 57(i) 62(i, ii) 70(ii) 71(ii, iv) 79(ii, iii) 94(vi) 95(ii, v) 96(ii) 97(v) 98(i–iv) 99(ii–iv) 105(v) 106(ii, v) 107(ii) 108(i, ii) 109(i, v) 110(iii) 112(iii) 117(v) 122(iv) 124(i) 127(ii)

The following Fs should be sharpened according to the MSS. as they represent original unflattened Es:

24(iv) 28(iv) 34(ii, 2nd F) 89(iii) 91(iii) 126(ii) 130(ii) 132(iv).

The Christ Church part-books frequently provide pauses at the end of verse and full sections; although the exact meaning of these is not known it is clear that they can not imply pauses as generally understood. In the closing bars of the work the word 'believers' alternates with 'sinners' inconsistently. Some editorial adjustment has been necessary here, especially as many part-books are ambiguous and the number of syllables occasionally exceeds the available notes. The text is by Dr. Goodman, Dean of Rochester.

Variants: 9.v.4: F$\sharp$(21) / 10.iv.3: B*m*–not C*m*(60) / 13.i–vi.3: see p. 218 / 18.i–vi: this section is compressed into 5 parts in 29372–6 and the Ch. Ch. part-books by combining Treble II and Alto I as a Quintus (until bar 21) / 18–26.v–vi: words omitted in error (21) / 19.iii.4: omit $\sharp$(57) / 23.i–ii.4: to*q*wards *q* men *m* good *m* will *c* to*m*wards *c*(56,29372) / 38.i.2: omit $\sharp$(21) / 45.i.5: and *q* mir*q*a*q*cles *c*. are *qmc*(21) / 46.i.3: *c* not *c*.(29372) / 55–76.i.3: omit viol part(56,29372) / 56.iv.1–2: *m* not *cc*(29374) / 57.i.4: omit $\sharp$(21) / 60.ii.3: omit$\sharp$(57) / 61.ii.3: fice *q.sq* a *qq* sac*qq*ri*c*(29376) / 62.ii.1: sac*qq*ri*c*(57) / 62.iv.4: omit $\sharp$(29374) / 63.iv.2: a *q* sac*q*ri*q*fice *q* for *q* sin *m*(60) / 70.ii.2: are *c* shak*c*en *c* 'are *cc*(29376) / 77.i.iv–v: *c.q* not *cc*(56,29372) / 80.ii.5: E*m* not B*m*(57,29376) / 81.ii.1: E*m* not C$\sharp$*m*(57,29376) / 85.i–iv: 'gored' not 'goring' (29372–6) / 87.iv.1–2: pricks *qq*(29375) / 87.ii.3: 'crown' not 'pricks' (59,29373) / 89.iii.1–5: pricks *q* of *q* thorns *qqc* (60) / 94.ii.1–2: *c.q* not *cc* (57,29376) / 94.ii.4: F$\sharp$*c* not E*c* (29375) / 96.i.3–4: *m* not *c.q*(21) (i.e. 'ascension' as 3 syllables) / 95.iii.1: as*c*cen*c*.si*q*on *c* as*c*cen*c*simon *c*(59) / 96.iii.3–4: *m* not *c.q*(29373) / 97.i.1–2: *m*. not *cm* (21) / 98.i.1: omit $\sharp$(56) / 99.iv.1–2: omit tie (60) / 99.i.3: B *c* not 4*sq*(21) / 100.i.1: *mc* not *m*.(56,29372) / 103.iv.4–8: lamb *q*. that *sq* sit*q*teth *sqsq*(60) / 105.i.1: *c* not *m*(56,29372) / 106.iii.3: sit*c*teth *c* on *c*(59) / 106.iii.3–4: *c* not *qq*(21) (i.e. 'sits' for 'sitteth') / 107.ii.3: *c* not *c*.(29376) / 108.ii.4: omit $\sharp$(29376) / 111.iv.4: be *q* he *q* that *q* com*q*eth *q*(60) / 112.i.2: bles*c*c.*sq*s*q*ed *q*(29372) / 112.iii.3: comes *q* in *c* the *qq*(59,29373) / 115.i.1: *c* not *m*(56,29372) / 118.ii.2,4,5: omit all $\sharp$s(21) / 118.ii.5: omit $\sharp$(57,29376) / 120.i.1: *c* not *m* (56,29372) / 120.ii.1: *c* not *m*(57,29376, so as to continue with the 1st Alto part) / 123.ii.8: all *c* be*q*liev*c*ers *c*. to *q* all *q* be*q*liev*q*gers *q* to *q* all *q*be*q*liev*c*.*q*ers *s(q)* to *q* all *q* be*q*(57, then p. 219 for variant ending) / 123.iv.1: laid *m* o*c*.pen *q* to *q* all *q* be*c*lievers *q (sic)* (29374) / 123.iv.1: and *q* heaven *c* laid *q* o*c*pen *q* to *q* all *q* be*c*liev*q*ers *c*(60) / 124–133.i–v: underlay is confused in all parts / 127.i: 21 introduces a Treble II on the 3rd quaver beat which doubles the 1st Alto part when the latter enters.

JOHN AMNER: **Remember not, Lord, our offences**

Sources: II and 266.

5.rh.up.3:♯ (266).

ADRIAN BATTEN: **O praise the Lord, all ye heathen**

Source: 235–41.

This is Batten's third setting of the text, as listed in the *Early English Church Music* inventory. No organ part has survived.

WALTER PORTER: **Praise the Lord**

Source: XXVI.

Porter explains in the preface to this work that the grouping of four demisemiquavers together on one note (as in bars 9, 11, 16 *et passim*) indicates a 'trillo'. The modern equivalent would presumably be a trill, without final turn.

WILLIAM CHILD: **O God, wherefore art thou absent from us?**

Source: 34–7: the version in 50, 64–5, 68 and 166–7 dates from post-Restoration times, and differs considerably from it.

John Bull
(By courtesy of the Faculty of Music, Oxford University)

T*

MODERN EDITIONS

COLLECTED EDITIONS

TUDOR CHURCH MUSIC, Volumes I–X (Oxford University Press, 1923–9)

    I   John Taverner (Part 1)
    II   William Byrd (Part 1)
    III John Taverner (Part 2)
    IV Orlando Gibbons
    V   Robert White
    VI Thomas Tallis
    VII William Byrd (Gradualia)
   VIII Thomas Tomkins (Part 1; Services)
    IX William Byrd (Masses, *Cantiones Sacrae* and Motets)
    X   Hugh Aston, John Marbeck and Osbert Parsley

EARLY ENGLISH CHURCH MUSIC, Volumes I– (Stainer and Bell, 1962–)

    I   Early Tudor Masses (Part 1)
    II   William Mundy (Latin Antiphons and Psalms)
    III Orlando Gibbons (Verse Anthems 1)
    IV Early Tudor Magnificats (Part 1)
    V   Thomas Tomkins (*Musica Deo Sacra* 1)
    VI Early Tudor Organ Music (Part 1)
    VII Robert Ramsey
   VIII Early Tudor Masses (Part 2)

MUSICA BRITANNICA (Stainer and Bell, 1951–

    V   Thomas Tomkins (Keyboard Music)
    VI John Dowland (Ayres for Four Voices)
   XIV John Bull (Keyboard Music, Part 1)
    XV Music of Scotland, 1500–1700
    XX Orlando Gibbons (Keyboard Music)
  XXIII Thomas Weelkes (Complete Anthems)

THE COLLECTED WORKS OF WILLIAM BYRD, 20 Volumes (Stainer and Bell, 1937–50)

THOMAS MORLEY. Collected Motets (Stainer and Bell, 1959)

SEPARATE PUBLICATIONS

(Items printed in **bold type** are included in this Volume)

(1) MUSIC TO ENGLISH TEXTS

ALISON, RICHARD (fl. 1600)

Behold, now praise the Lord	SB.
O Lord, bow down thine ear	SB.
The sacred choir of angels	SB.

AMNER, JOHN (c. 1585–1641)

A stranger here	SB.
Away with weak complainings	SB.
Come, let's rejoice	SB.
He that descended, man to be	Y.
Lift up your heads	OUP.
Love we in one consenting	OUP.
O come, O come, thou Spirit divinest	Y.
O ye little flock	CMS.(OUP.)
Remember not, Lord our offences	BP.

ANON.

O Lord, the maker (Wanley MSS.)	OUP.
This is the day	OUP.

BATESON, THOMAS (c. 1570–1630)

Holy, Lord God almighty	N.

BATTEN, ADRIAN (before 1590–c. 1637)

Communion; The Short Service	CMS.(OUP.)
Service for Men (Magnificat and Nunc dimittis)	CMS.(OUP.)
Fourth Service (Magnificat and Nunc dimittis)	OUP.
Deliver us, O Lord our God	OUP.
Haste thee, O God	OUP.
Hear my prayer, O God	OUP.
Hear my prayer, O Lord	S.
Hear the prayers, O our God	S.
Let my complaint	N. OUP.
Lord, we beseech thee	OUP.
Lord, who shall dwell	O.
My soul truly waiteth	O.
O clap your hands together	S.
O Lord, thou hast searched me out	S.
O praise the Lord, all ye heathen	OUP.
O praise the Lord, all ye heathen	BP.
O sing joyfully	OUP.
Out of the deep	S.

Sing we merrily   N.
We beseech thee, almighty God   S.
When the Lord turned again   OUP.

BEVIN, ELWAY (fl. 1575–after 1634)
    Morning and Evening Service (Te Deum, Bene-   BCM.
      dictus, Kyrie, Creed, Magnificat, Nunc dimittis)

BRYNE, ALBERTUS (?–1668?)
    Morning and Evening Service (Te Deum, Jubilate,   N.
      Sanctus, Kyrie, Creed, Magnificat, Nunc dimittis)

BULL, JOHN (c. 1563–1628)
    Almighty God, who by the leading of a star   OUP.
    Attend unto my tears   SB.
    In the departure of the Lord   BP. SB.
    O Lord my God   C.
    O Lord, turn not away thy face   SB.

BYRD, WILLIAM (1543–1623)
    The Great Service (Venite, Te Deum, Benedictus,   OUP. SB.(X)*
      Kyrie, Creed, Magnificat, **Nunc dimittis**)   BP.
    The Short Service (Te Deum, Benedictus, Kyrie,   OUP. SB.(X)
      Creed, Sanctus, Magnificat, Nunc dimittis)
    The Third Service (Magnificat, Nunc dimittis)   OUP. SB.(X)
    Preces, Responses and Litany   CMS. OUP. SB.(X)
    Alack, when I look back   SB.(XI)
    An earthly tree   SB.(XI)
    Arise, Lord, into thy rest   SB.[XI](XIV)
    Arise, O Lord, why sleepest thou   OUP. SB.(III)[XI]
    Attend mine humble prayer   SB.(XIII)
    Be unto me [O Lord] a tower   N. SB.(XI)
    Behold, O God   SB.(XI)
    Blessed is he that fears   SB.(XII)
    Bow thine ear   CMS.(OUP)
                                                        SB.(II)[XI]

    Christ rising again   L. SB.(XIII)
    Come help, O God   CMS.(OUP) N.
                                                        SB.(II)[XI]

    Come let us rejoice   OUP. SB.[XI] (XIV)
    From depth of sin   SB.(XIII)
    From Virgin's womb   SB.[XI](XIII)

* Roman numerals refer to the Volume in the *Collected Works*: items in square brackets
have been transposed for modern performance.

Have mercy upon me	SB.[XI](XIV)
Help, Lord, for wasted are those men	SB.(XII)
How long shall mine enemies	SB.(XI)
If that a sinner's sighs	SB.(XII)
I have been young	SB.(XIV)
I laid me down to rest	N. SB.(XI)
Lift up your heads	SB.(I)
Look down, O Lord	N. SB.(XI)
Lord, hear my prayer	SB.(XIII)
Lord, in thy rage	SB.(XIII)
Lord, in thy wrath correct me not	SB.(XIII)
Lord, in thy wrath reprove me not	SB.(XII)
Make ye joy to God	SB.[XI](XIV)
Mine eyes with fervency	SB.(XII)
My soul oppressed with care	SB.(XII)
O God, give ear	C. SB.(XII)
O God that guides the cheerful sun	SB.(XIV)
O God, the proud are risen	SB.(XI)
O God, which art most merciful	SB.(XIII)
O God, whom our offences	OUP. SB.(XI)
O Lord, make thy servant Elizabeth	SB.(XI)
O Lord, my God	SB.(XIII)
O Lord, turn thy wrath (Ne irascaris)	OUP.
	BP. (another version)
O Lord, who in thy sacred tent	SB.(XII)
O praise our Lord, ye saints	SB.(XI)
Praise our Lord, all ye Gentiles	SB.(XIV)
Prevent us, O Lord	CMS. OUP. SB.(XI)
Rejoice, rejoice	SB.(XIII)
Right blest are they	SB.(XIII)
Sing joyfully	BP. N. SB.(XI)
Sing we merrily	SB.[XI](XIV)
Sing ye to our Lord	SB.[XI](XIV)
Teach me, O Lord	BP. CMS.(OUP)
This day Christ was born	SB.[XI](XIV)
Turn our captivity, O Lord	SB.[XI](XIV)
Unto the hills	SB.(XIII)
What unacquainted cheerful voice	SB(XV)
When Israel came out of Egypt	SB.(X)

CAUSTUN, THOMAS (before 1535–69)

Service 'For Children' (Te Deum, Benedictus, Kyrie, Creed, Magnificat, Nunc dimittis)	N. OUP.
Service 'for men' (Nunc dimittis)	BP.
Rejoice in the Lord	Y.

CHILD, WILLIAM (1606–1697)
>   Service in D ('sharp') (Te Deum, Jubilate, Kyrie,   BCM.
>   Creed, Magnificat, Nunc dimittis)
>   Service in E (minor) ('with the lesser third') (Te   BCM.
>   Deum, Jubilate, Kyrie, Creed, Magnificat, Nunc
>   dimittis)
>   If the Lord himself   N.
>   **O God, wherefore art thou absent from us?**   BP.
>   O Lord, grant the King a long life   N.
>   O pray for the peace of Jerusalem   N.
>   Praise the Lord   N.
>   Sing we merrily   N.
>   Turn thou us   OUP.

COPERARIO, JOHN (c. 1575–1626)
>   I'll lay [lie] me down to sleep   N.

DOWLAND, JOHN (1562–1626)
>   An heart that's broken   N.
>   'Seven Hymn Tunes'   OUP.
>   See also *Musica Britannica*, Volume VI

EAST, MICHAEL (c. 1580–1648)
>   As they departed   MAS.
>   Blow out the trumpet   MAS.
>   Haste thee, O God   SB.
>   How shall a young man   MAS.
>   I have roared   MAS.
>   O clap your hands   SB.
>   Sing we merrily   MAS.
>   Turn thy face   MAS.
>   When David heard   S. SB.
>   When Israel came out of Egypt   OUP. SB.

FARMER, JOHN (before 1575–?)
>   **The Lord's Prayer**   BP.
>   O Lord, of whom I do depend   SB.

FARRANT, JOHN (1575–1618)
>   Morning and Evening Service (Te Deum, Jubilate,   OUP.
>   Magnificat, Nunc dimittis)

FARRANT, RICHARD (before 1535–1581)
>   Morning and Evening Service
>   (Te Deum, Benedictus, Magnificat, Nunc dimittis)   OUP.
>   (Kyrie, Creed)   BCM.
>   Call to remembrance   OUP.
>   **Hide not thou thy face**   BP. OUP.
>   **Lord, for thy tender mercy's sake**   BP. N. OUP.
>   (also attributed to John Hilton the Elder)

FERRABOSCO, ALPHONSO (ii) (1575–1628)
        In death no man remembreth thee   N.
        In thee, O Lord   SB.

FORD, THOMAS (*c.* 1580–1648)
        Almighty God, who hast me brought   N.
        Let God arise   MAS.
        Not unto us   N.

GIBBONS, ORLANDO (1583–1625)
        The Short Service (Te Deum, Benedictus, Magni-   BP. OUP.
          ficat, **Nunc dimittis**)
        The Short Service (Kyrie, Creed)   BCM.
        The Verse Service (Magnificat, Nunc dimittis)   OUP.
        Almighty and everlasting God   OUP.
        Almighty God, who by thy Son   OUP.
        Behold, thou hast made my days   OUP.
        Blessed be the Lord God   N.
        Deliver us, O Lord   N.
        Glorious and powerful God   N.
        God is gone up (part II of 'O clap your hands')
        Great King of Gods (see 'Great Lord of Lords')
        Great Lord of Lords   SB.
        Hosanna to the Son of David   N. OUP.
        If ye be risen   N.
        Lift up your heads   N. OUP.
        O all true faithful hearts   N.
        O clap your hands   N. OUP.
        O God, the King of glory   OUP.
        O Lord, how do my woes increase   N.
        O Lord, I lift my heart   N.
        O Lord, increase my faith (see Loosemore)
        O Lord, in thy wrath rebuke me not   BP. OUP.
        See, see, the Word is incarnate   BP. SB.
        The eyes of all wait   N.
        This is the record of John   N. OUP.
        See also *Tudor Church Music*, Volume IV and *Early
          English Church Music*, Volume III.

GILES, NATHANIEL (*c.* 1558–1633)
        God which as at this time   OUP.
        Out of the deep   OUP.

HILTON, JOHN (The Elder) (before 1565–after 1612)
        Call to remembrance   OUP.
        Lord, for thy tender mercy's sake—
          see RICHARD FARRANT

HOOPER, EDMUND (*c.* 1553–1621)
        The Full Service (Magnificat, Nunc dimittis)   OUP.
        The Verse Service (Magnificat, Nunc dimittis)   OUP.
        Behold, it is Christ   S.
        Teach me thy way, O Lord   CMS.(OUP.)

HUNT, THOMAS (fl. 1600)
        Morning and Evening Service (Venite, Te Deum,   OUP.
             Benedictus, Magnificat, Nunc dimittis)

JONES, ROBERT (fl. 1600)
        Lament my soul   AMP.

LAWES, WILLIAM (1602–1645)
        The Lord is my light   BCM.

LOOSEMORE, HENRY (?–1670)
        Litany   N.
        O Lord, increase my faith (attr. O. Gibbons)   L. N. OUP.

LUPO, THOMAS (?–1628)
        Out of the deep   OUP.

MERBECKE, JOHN (*c.* 1510–1585)
        The Booke of Common Praier Noted (**Nunc dimit-**   BP.
        tis, Communion Anthem and Agnus Dei
        only)
        See also *Tudor Church Music*, Volume X

MILTON, JOHN (1563–1647)
        I am the resurrection   WP.
        If that a sinner's sighs   WP.
        O had I wings like to a dove   WP.
        O Lord, behold my miseries   WP.
        Thou God of might   WP.
        When David heard   WP.

MORLEY, THOMAS (1557–1603)
        The First Service (Magnificat, Nunc dimittis)   OUP.
        The Short Service (Magnificat, Nunc dimittis)   OUP.
        The Burial Service (I am the Resurrection; I know   BCM.
           that my Redeemer liveth; We brought nothing
           into this world; Man that is born of woman; In
           the midst of life; Thou knowest, Lord; I heard a
           voice from heaven)
        Preces and Responses   CMS.(OUP.)
        Nolo mortem peccatoris   BP. OUP. SB.
        Out of the deep (Full Anthem: adapted from 'De   SB.
        profundis')
        Out of the deep (Verse Anthem)   BP. N. OUP.
        See also Morley's *Collected Motets* (SB.)

MUDD, JOHN (?–1631?)
    Let thy merciful ears   OUP.
    O God, who hast prepared   N. OUP.

MUNDY, JOHN (?–1630)
    Hear my prayer, O Lord   OUP.
    In deep distress   OUP.
    Sing joyfully   OUP.
    Sing ye unto the Lord   OUP.
    See also: *English Madrigalists*, Volume 35B   SB.

MUNDY, WILLIAM (*c.* 1530–1591)
    The First Service (Magnificat, Nunc dimittis)   N.
    Ah, helpless wretch   BP.
    O Lord, the maker of all things   BP. OUP.
    See also *Early English Church Music*, Volume II

NICHOLSON, RICHARD (?–1639)
    O pray for the peace of Jerusalem   OUP.
    When Jesus sat at meat   OUP.

PARSLEY, OSBERT (1511–1585)
    Morning and Evening Service (Te Deum, Bene-   OUP.
        dictus, Magnificat, Nunc dimittis)
    See also *Tudor Church Music*, Volume X

PARSONS, ROBERT (?–1570)
    The First Service (**Nunc dimittis**)   BP.
    Deliver me from mine enemies   N.

PARSONS, WILLIAM (*c.* 1515–after 1561)
    In trouble and in thrall   BP.

PATRICK, NATHANIEL (?–1595)
    Morning and Evening Service (Te Deum, Bene-   CMS.(OUP.)
        dictus, Magnificat, Nunc dimittis)

PEERSON, MARTIN (*c.* 1580–1650)
    Blow out the trumpet   S.
    Lord, ever bridle my desires   S.
    Man, dream no more   S.
    O God, that no time dost despise   S.
    O God, when thou wentest forth   S.
    O let me at thy footstool fall   S.

PILKINGTON, FRANCIS (?–1638)
    Care for thy soul   SB.
    Hidden, O Lord   AMP.
    High, mighty God   N.
    O gracious God of heaven   SB.
    O praise the Lord, all ye heathen   SB.

PORTER, WALTER (*c.* 1595–1659)
  Praise the Lord   BP.

RAMSEY, ROBERT (fl. 1640)
  Almighty and everlasting God   S.
  God, who as upon this day   S.
  My song shall be alway   S.
  O come let us sing   S.
  When David heard   S.
  See also *Early English Church Music*, Volume VII

RAVENSCROFT, THOMAS (*c.* 1590–*c.* 1633)
  Ah, helpless soul   CMS.(OUP.)
  O Jesu meek   CMS.(OUP.)
  Remember God's goodness   N.

[REDFORD, JOHN (?–1547)]
  Rejoice in the Lord alway (attribution uncertain) OUP.

ROGERS, BENJAMIN (1614–1698)
  Morning and Evening Service in D ('with the BCM.
    greater third') (Te Deum, Jubilate, Kyrie,
    Creed, Magnificat, Nunc dimittis)
  Evening Service in A minor (Magnificat, Nunc N.
    dimittis)
  Evening Service in F (Magnificat, Nunc dimittis) BA.
  Behold, how good and joyful   O.
  Behold, now praise the Lord   O.
  Lord, who shall dwell   N.
  O give thanks   O.
  O pray for the peace of Jerusalem   N.
  Teach me, O Lord   O.

SHEPHERD, JOHN (*c.* 1520–1563?)
  Haste thee, O God   N. OUP.
  I give you a new commandment (attributed to Tallis) OUP.
  O Lord of hosts   CMS.(OUP.)
  Steven first after Christ (see Hawkins, Sir John,
    History of Music, Vol. II)

SMITH, WILLIAM (fl. 1630)
  Preces and Responses   CMS.(OUP.)

STONE, ROBERT (1516–1613)
  The Lord's Prayer   BP. N.

TALLIS, THOMAS (*c.* 1505–1585)
  The Short Service (Te Deum, Benedictus, Kyrie, BCM.
    Creed, Magnificat, Nunc dimittis)
  The Short Service (Magnificat, Nunc dimittis) OUP.

Te Deum for Five Voices	OUP.
Preces and Responses	CMS.(OUP.)
Litany	N.
Blessed be thy name	OUP.
Hear my prayer	OUP.
Hear the voice and prayer	N.
I call and cry (O sacrum convivium)	OUP.
I give you a new commandment	OUP.
If ye love me	BP. OUP.
O God, be merciful	OUP.
O Lord, give thy Holy Spirit	OUP.
O Lord, in thee is all my trust	OUP.
Purge me, O Lord	OUP.
This is my commandment	OUP.
Wherewithal shall a young man cleanse his way? Festal Psalm	BP.
With all our hearts and mouths (Salvator mundi)	BP. CH. (another version)

See also *Tudor Church Music*, Volume VI.

TOMKINS, THOMAS (1572–1656)

Evening Service in C (Magnificat, Nunc dimittis)	N.
The Second Service (Te Deum, Jubilate, Magnificat, Nunc dimittis)	OUP.
The Third Service (Magnificat, Nunc dimittis)	OUP.
The Fourth Service (**Nunc dimittis**)	BP.
The Fifth Service (Magnificat, Nunc dimittis)	OUP.
Preces and Responses	CMS.(OUP.)
Almighty and everlasting God	H.
Almighty God, the fountain	S.
Arise, O Lord, into thy resting place	BP.
Behold, the hour cometh	S.
God, who as at this time	H.
Great and marvellous	OUP.
Hear my prayer	S.
He that hath pity	N.
I am the Resurrection	N. OUP.
I heard a voice	N.
My beloved spake	S.
My shepherd is the living Lord	SB.
O give thanks	OUP.
O God, wonderful art thou	OUP.
O how amiable are thy dwellings	CMS.(OUP.)
O Lord, I have loved	H.
O praise the Lord, all ye heathen	OUP.

O pray for the peace of Jerusalem   OUP.
O sing unto the Lord a new song   S.
Praise the Lord, O my soul   OUP.
Then David mourned   H. S.
Thou art my King, O God   AMP. SB.
When David heard   SB.
Woe is me   SB.
See also *Tudor Church Music*, Volume VIII, and *Early English Church Music*, Volume V.

TYE, CHRISTOPHER (*c.* 1505–1572)
    Magnificat and Nunc dimittis (also attributed to   OUP.
       Parsley)
    Nunc dimittis   BP.
    Give alms of thy goods   OUP.
    I will exalt [extol] thee   OUP.
    O come, ye servants of the Lord   SB.
    O God, be merciful   OUP.
    Praise [ye] the Lord, ye children   OUP.
    Sing unto the Lord   OUP.

WARD, JOHN (fl. 1620)
    The First Service (Magnificat, Nunc dimittis)   N.
    O let me tread   CMS.(OUP.)
    O Lord, consider my complaint   N.

WEELKES, THOMAS (*c.* 1575–1623)
    The Short Service (Te Deum, Benedictus, Magni-   SB.
       ficat, Nunc dimittis)
    Magnificat and Nunc dimittis (in Five Parts)   OUP.
    Magnificat and Nunc dimittis (in Seven Parts)   OUP.
    Magnificat and Nunc dimittis ('for Trebles')   SB.
    Alleluia, I heard a voice   SB.
    All people, clap your hands   MAS.
    Give ear, O Lord   BP. SB.
    Gloria in excelsis Deo   BP. OUP. SB.
    Hosanna to the Son of David   OUP.
    Let thy merciful ears (See MUDD)
    O how amiable   OUP.
    O Jonathan, woe is me   AMP. S.
    O Lord, arise into thy resting place   OUP.
    O Lord, grant the King a long life   OUP.
    O mortal man   C.
    When David heard   AMP. N.
    See also *Musica Britannica*, Volume XXIII (Complete Anthems).

WHITE, ROBERT (*c.* 1535–1574)
       O how glorious   WI.
       O praise God in his holiness   OUP.
       The Lord bless us   WI.
       See also *Tudor Church Music*, Volume V.

WILBYE, JOHN (1574–1638)
       I am quite tired   SB.
       O God the rock   N. SB.
       O Lord, turn not thy face   N.

(2) MUSIC TO LATIN TEXTS

BYRD, WILLIAM (1543–1623)
       Mass for Three Voices (Kyrie, Gloria, Creed,   CH. SB.(I)*
          Sanctus, Agnus Dei)
       Mass for Four Voices (**Kyrie**, Gloria, Creed, Sanc-   CH. SB.(I) BP.
          tus, Agnus Dei)
       Mass for Five Voices (Kyrie, Gloria, Creed, Sanc-   CH. SB.(I)
          tus, Agnus Dei)

       Alleluia, ascendit Deus   SB.(VIII)
       Alleluia, cognoverunt discipuli   N. SB. (VI)
       Aspice, Domine   SB.(I)
       Assumpta est Maria   C. SB.(IV)
       Attolite portas   SB.(I)
       Ave Maria, gratia plena   BP. CH. SB.(IV)
       Ave Regina   CH. SB.(V)
       Ave verum corpus   BP. OUP. SB.(V)
       Beata es, Virgo Maria   CH. SB.(IV)
       Beata viscera Mariae Virginis   CH. SB.(IV)
       Cantate Domino   OUP. SB.(III)
       Christe, qui lux es   OUP. SB.(VIII)
       Christus resurgens   CH. SB.(V)
       Civabit eos   CH.
       Civitas sancti tui   CH.
       Confirma hoc, Deus   CH. N. SB.(VII)
       De lamentatione   SB.(VIII)
       Dies sanctificatus   N. SB.(VI)
       Ego sum panis vivus   CH. SB.(VI)
       Emendemus in melius   SB.(I)
       Exsurge, quare obdormis   OUP.
       Felix es, sacra Virgo   SB.(IV)
       Haec dies   N. OUP. SB.(III)(VI)
       Justorum animae   SB.(IV)
       Laetentur coeli   N. OUP.

* The Roman numerals refer to the Volume in the *Collected Works*

Laudibus in sanctis   SB.(III)*
Libera me   SB.(I)
Lumen ad revelationem   N.
Miserere mei   OUP. SB.(III)(VIII)
Ne irascaris (O Lord, turn thy wrath)   BP.
Non vos relinquam   CH. SB.(VII)
O Lux beata Trinitas   SB.(I)
O magnum mysterium   CH. SB.(VI)
O quam gloriosum   OUP. SB.(II)
O quam suavis   CH. N. SB.(VI)
O rex gloriae   CH. SB.(VII)
O sacrum convivium   CH. N. SB.(V)
Oculi omnium   SB.(V)
Peccantem me quotidie   SB.(I)
Psallite Domino   SB.(VII)
Rorate coeli   OUP. SB.(IV)
Sacerdotes Domini   OUP. SB.(V)
Salve Regina   CH. SB.(III)
Salve, sancta parens   CH. SB.(IV)
Senex puerum portabat   CH. N. SB.(IV)
Siderum rector   SB.(I)
Surge illuminare   N. SB.(VI)
Te deprecor   SB.(I)
Terra tremuit   N. SB.(VI)
Tu es pastor ovium   CH. SB.(VII)
Tu es Petrus   SB.(VII)
Tui sunt coeli   N. SB.(VI)
Veni, Sancte Spiritus   SB.(VII)
Victimae paschali   OUP. SB.(VI)

DERING, RICHARD (c. 1580–1630)
Factum est silentium   BP.
Jesu, summa benignitas   CH.
Quem vidistis, pastores   CH. N.

JOHNSON, ROBERT (c. 1490–c. 1560)
Dum transisset Sabbatum   CH.

KIRBYE, GEORGE (?–1634)
Vox in Rama   SB.

LUPO, THOMAS (?–1628)
O vos omnes   CH.

MORLEY, THOMAS (1557–1603)
Agnus Dei   SB.
De profundis clamavi   OUP. SB.

* The Roman numerals refer to the Volume in the *Collected Works*.

Domine, dominus noster	SB.
Domine, fac mecum	N. SB.
Domine, non est exaltatum	SB.
Ehu, sustulerunt Dominum	N. SB.
Laboravi in gemitu meo	OUP. SB.
See also Morley's *Collected Motets* (SB.).	

OKELAND, ROBERT (fl. 1560)

Kyrie	CH. SB.

PHILIPS, PETER (*c*. 1565–*c*. 1635)

Alma redemptoris mater	CH.
Ascendit Deus	BP. OUP.
Ave Regina	CH.
Cantantibus organis	N.
Elegi abjectus esse	CH.
Gaudent in coelis	N.
Ne reminiscaris, Domine	N.
O virum mirabilem	CH.
Regina coeli	CH.
Surgens Jesus	N.
Viae Sion lugent	N.

SHEPHERD, JOHN (?–1563?)

Playnsong Mass for a Mene	CH.
The French Mass	CH.
Alleluia, confitemini Domino	N.
Haec dies	CH.

TALLIS, THOMAS (*c*. 1505–1585)

Audivi vocem	OUP.
Dum transisset Sabbatum	CH.
Gloria Patri	N.
In jejunio et fletu	CH.
In manus tuas	SB.
Lamentationes	OUP.
Laudate Dominum	CH.
O nata lux	OUP.
O sacrum convivium	SB.
O salutaris hostia	CH.
Salvator mundi (With all our hearts)	BP. (another version)
Rubum quem viderat	CH.
Salve, intemerata Virgo	OUP.
Spem in alium (40 parts)	OUP.
Te lucis ante terminum	N.
See also *Tudor Church Music*, Volume VI.	

TYE, CHRISTOPHER (*c.* 1505–1572)

Euge Bone Mass	WI.
Omnes gentes, plaudite	CH.
Ruvum quem viderat	CH.

WHITE, ROBERT (*c.* 1535–1574)

Christe, qui lux es et dies	BP. CH. OUP.
Lamentations	SB.
Libera me, Domine	OUP.
Precamur, sancte Domine. See Christe, qui lux es et dies.	

KEY

AMP.	Associated Music Publishers, New York
BA.	Banks & Son, York
BCM.	Boyce's Cathedral Music
BP.	Blandford Press
BUA.	Burns & Allen, New York
C.	Curwen
CH.	Chester
CMS.	Church Music Society Reprints (OUP.)
H.	Hinrichsen
L.	Lawson Gould, New York
MAS.	Musical Antiquarian Society (Chappell)
N.	Novello
O.	Ollivier
OUP.	Oxford University Press
S.	Schott
SB.	Stainer & Bell
WI.	Joseph Williams (Galliard)
WP.	Williams & Parker (Old English Edition)
Y.	Year Book Press (Ascherberg, Hopwood & Crew)

The list of Music to English texts has been compiled from 'The Sources of English Sacred Music' by R. T. Daniel and P. G. le Huray; (published in the *Early English Church Music series*: Stainer & Bell).

The list of Music to Latin texts is taken from Denis Stevens' *Tudor Church Music*, (Faber and Faber, 1961)

The title page from *Musica Deo Sacra* by Thomas
Tomkins, published posthumously in 1668
(By kind permission of the Governing Body of Christ Church,
Oxford)

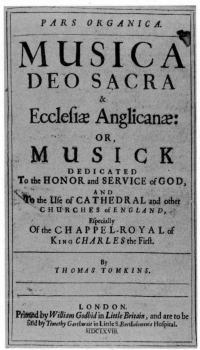

BIBLIOGRAPHY

Daniel, R. T. and le Huray, P. G.: 'The Sources of English Sacred Music, *c.* 1550–
1650, to be published in the *Early English Church Music* Series, 1966.

Davies, G.: *The Early Stuarts (1603–1660)*. (Oxford University Press, 1959.)

Dickens, A. G.: *The English Reformation*. (Batsford, 1964.)

Dixon, R. W.: *History of the Church of England*. (Oxford University Press.)

Harrison, F. Ll.: *Music in Medieval Britain*. (Routledge, 1958.)

Fellowes, E. H.: *English Cathedral Music*. (Methuen, 1946.); *William Byrd*. (Oxford
University Press, 1936.); *Orlando Gibbons*. (Oxford University Press, 1951.)

Lafontaine, H. C. de: *The King's Musick*. (Novello, 1909.)

le Huray, P. G.: *Church Music in England, 1549–1644*. (Herbert Jenkins, to be published
in 1966.)

Morley, Thomas: *A Plain and Easy Introduction to Practical Music*, ed. A. Harman.
(Dent, 1952.)

Rimbault, E. F.: 'The Old Cheque Book of the Chapel Royal'. (Camden Society, New
Series III, 1872.)

Stevens, D.: *Tudor Church Music*. (Faber and Faber, 1961.); *Thomas Tomkins*.
(Macmillan, 1957.)

Usher, R. G.: *The Reconstruction of the English Church*. (Appleton, 1910.)

Woodfill, W. L.: *Musicians in English Society*. (Princeton University Press, 1953.)

DISCOGRAPHY*

COMPOSER	TITLE	ARTISTS	RECORD NO.
AMNER, JOHN (*c.* 1585-1641)	*O ye little flock* (from 'Sacred Hymns'—1615)	Renaissance Singers	RG148 **ZRG5148**
BARCROFT, THOMAS (*fl.* 1535)	*O Lord, we beseech thee*	Ely Cathedral Choir	AVM015
BATTEN, ADRIAN (before 1590-*c.* 1637)	*Deliver us, O Lord*	Christ Church Choir	ECB3159 **DS6059**
	Evening Service No. 4	Peterborough Cathedral Choir	RG318 **ZRG5318**
	Hear my prayer	Christ Church Choir	ECB3159 **DS6059**
		Peterborough Cathedral Choir	RG318 **ZRG5318**
	O clap your hands together	Peterborough Cathedral Choir	RG318 **ZRG5318**
	O Lord, thou hast searched me out	Peterborough Cathedral Choir	RG318 **ZRG5318**
	O praise the Lord	King's College Choir	RG99
		Christ Church Choir	ECB3159 **DS6059**
	O sing joyfully	Peterborough Cathedral Choir	RG318 **ZRG5318**
	Out of the deep	Peterborough Cathedral Choir	RG318 **ZRG5318**
BYRD, WILLIAM (1543-1623)	*Magnificat* and *Nunc dimittis* (from the Great Service)	King's College Choir	RG226 **ZRG5226**
	Magnificat and *Nunc dimittis* (from the Second Service)	Westminster Abbey Choir	RG371 **ZRG5371**
	Mass for 5 voices	King's College Choir	RG226 **ZRG5226**
		Montreal Bach Choir	DL880
	Mass for 4 voices (Kyrie)	King's College Choir	RG362 **ZRG5362**
		Montreal Bach Choir	DL880
		Westminster Abbey Choir	APM14301 **SAPM198301**
	Mass for 3 voices	King's College Choir	RG362 **ZRG5362**
	An earthly tree	Renaissance Singers	RG148 **ZRG5148**
		Ely Cathedral Choir	eaf8 **zfa8**
	Ave Verum Corpus	St. Paul's Cathedral Choir	33CX1193
		King's College Choir	RG226 **ZRG5226**
		Ely Cathedral Choir	AVM015
	Bow Thine ear	Christ Church Choir	ECB3159 **DS6059**
	Haec dies	King's College Choir	RG120
		St. Paul's Cathedral Choir	HMV (History of Music in Sound) HLP9
	Hodie beata Virgo Maria	Magdalen College Choir	AVM009
	Lullaby, my sweet little baby song	Abbey Singers	AXA4518**SXA4518**
	Non nobis, Domine	Deller Consort	TFL6022
	Prevent us, O Lord	Christ Church Choir	ECB3159 **DS6059**
	Sing joyfully	Christ Church Choir	ECB3159 **DS6059**

* Discography compiled by the General Editors. A recording of music from this volume, by the Choir of Westminster Abbey, has been made by HMV.

CAMPIAN, THOMAS (1567–1620)	*Terra tremuit*	Ely Cathedral Choir	DS6059 **ECB3159**
	Never weather beaten sail	Northern Consort	rrt1001
		Wilfred Brown and D. Channor	CLP1633 **CSD1487**
		Alfred Deller, D. Dupre	OL50102
	Most sweet and pleasing are thy ways, O God (song)	Alfred Deller, D. Dupre	OL50102
CAUSTUN, THOMAS (before 1535–1569)	*Rejoice in the Lord*	Renaissance Singers	RG148 **ZRG5148**
DEERING, RICHARD (c. 1580–1630)	*Ave verum corpus*	Peterborough Cathedral Choir	RG318 **ZRG5318**
	Contristatus est rex David	Peterborough Cathedral Choir	RG318 **ZRG5318**
	Duo seraphin	Peterborough Cathedral Choir	RG318 **ZRG5318**
	Factum est silentium	Peterborough Cathedral Choir	RG318 **ZRG5318**
	Gaudent in coelis	Peterborough Cathedral Choir	RG318 **ZRG5318**
	Jesu dulcis memoria	Magdalen College Choir	AVM009
	O bone Jesu	Peterborough Cathedral Choir	RG318 **ZRG5318**
		New College Choir	avme008
DOWLAND, JOHN (1562–1626)	*Come, Holy Ghost*	Hilversum Vocal Ensemble	(R)643225
EAST, MICHAEL (c.1580–1648)	*When Israel came out of Egypt*	New York Pro Musica Motet Choir	AXA4524 **SXA4524**
FARRANT, RICHARD (before 1535–1581)	*Hide not thy Face, O Lord*	Welsh Festival Choir	ECB3145
		King's College Choir	RG365 **ZRG5365**
GIBBONS, ORLANDO (1583–1625)	*Almighty and everlasting God*	King's College Choir	RG80
		Schola Cantorum Basiliensis	APM14056
	Behold, thou hast made my days	Hampstead Church Choir	HMV (History of Music in Sound) HLP9
	Glorious and powerful God	King's College Choir	RG151 **ZRG5151**
	God is gone up	King's College Choir	RG80
	Great King of Gods	Westminster Abbey Choir	7eg8042
	Hosanna to the Son of David	King's College Choir	RG80
	O clap your hands	King's College Choir	RG80
	O God the King of Glory	King's College Choir	RG80
	O Lord, I lift my heart to thee	Schola Cantorum Basiliensis	APM14056
	O Lord, in thy wrath rebuke me not	King's College Choir	RG80
	O Lord, increase my faith	King's College Choir	RG80
		Schola Cantorum Basiliensis	APM14056
	O my love, how comely now	Schola Cantorum Basiliensis	APM14056
	See, see, the word is incarnate	King's College Choir	RG151 **ZRG5151**
	Song of Moses (No. 1)	King's College Choir	RG151 **ZRG5151**
	This is the record of John	Schola Cantorum Basiliensis	APM14056
		Renaissance Singers	RG148 **ZRG5148**
		King's College Choir	RG151 **ZRG5151**
	Thus angels sung	Schola Cantorum Basiliensis	APM14056
	Evensong for Whitsunday and Ascension Day (excerpts)	King's College Choir	RG80
	O word immortal	St. Michael's Singers	edp212
	Preces and Responses for Whitsunday (and Psalm 145) (2nd setting)	King's College Choir	RG151 **ZRG5151**
	Veni Creator	King's College Choir	RG80
		Schola Cantorum Basiliensis	APM14056
	Te Deum and Jubilate from the Verse Service	King's College Choir	RG151 **ZRG5151**
	Magnificat and Nunc dimittis from the Verse Service	King's College Choir	RG80
MORLEY, THOMAS (1557–1603)	*Agnus Dei*	St. Paul's Cathedral Choir	HMV (History of Music in Sound) HLP9
		Ely Cathedral Choir	AVM015

MUDD, THOMAS (c.1560–1632)	*Let thy merciful ears, O Lord*	Magdalen College Choir	AVM009
MUNDY, WILLIAM (c.1530–1591)	*O Lord, the maker of all things.*	Welsh Festival Choir	ECB3145
NICHOLSON, RICHARD (?–1639)	*O pray for the peace*	Magdalen College Choir	AVM009
PEERSON, MARTIN (c.1580–1650)	*Blow out the trumpet*	New York Pro Musica Motet Choir	AXA4524 **SXA4524**
PHILIPS, PETER (c.1560–1629)	*Surgens Jesus*	Ely Cathedral Choir	AVM 015
TALLIS, THOMAS (c.1505–1585)	*Adesto nunc propitius*	St. Paul's Cathedral Choir	HMV (History of Music in Sound). HLP9
	Audivi vocem	St. John's College Choir	RG237 **ZRG5237**
	In jejunio et fletu	St. John's College Choir	RG237 **ZRG5237**
	Te Deum (5-part)	St. John's College Choir	RG237 **ZRG5237**
	Why fumeth in fight	St. Michael's Choir	edp212
	O nata lux	Deller Consort	TFL6022
TOMKINS, THOMAS (1572–1656)	*Responses, Psalm 15, Te Deum and Benedictus* (from the First Service)	Magdalen College Choir	RG249 **ZRG5249**
	Preces and Responses (from the First Service)	King's College Choir	RG120
	Above the stars my Saviour dwells	Magdalen College Choir	RG249 **ZRG5249**
	Almighty God, the fountain	Magdalen College Choir	AVM009
	Holy, holy, holy	Magdalen College Choir	RG249 **ZRG5249**
	My Shepherd is the living Lord	Magdalen College Choir	RG249 **ZRG5249**
	Turn unto the Lord	Magdalen College Choir	RG249 **ZRG5249**
	When David heard that Absalom was slain	Magdalen College Choir	RG249 **ZRG5249**
WEELKES, THOMAS (c.1575–1623)	*Alleluia, I heard a voice*	St. John's College Choir	RG237 **ZRG5237**
	Give ear, O Lord	St. John's College Choir	RG237 **ZRG5237**
	Hosanna to the Son of David	St. Paul's Cathedral Choir	33CX1193
		St. John's College Choir	RG237 **ZRG5237**
		Ely Cathedral Choir	AVM015
	When David heard	St. John's College Choir	RG237 **ZRG5237**
		New York Pro Musica Motet Choir	AXA4524 **SXA4524**
	Nunc Dimittis (In medio chori)	St. John's College Choir	RG237 **ZRG5237**

KEY

ALP (HLP)	HMV.
APM **SAPM**	ARCHIVE
AVM	ALPHA
avme	ALPHA
AXA **SAXA**	BRUNSWICK
CLP **CSD**	HMV.
DL	VOX
eaf **zfa**	ARGO
ECB **DS**	DELYSE
edp	DELYSE
OL.	OISEAU-LYRE
RG **ZRG**	ARGO
rrt	CAMPION
(R) 640000 (Series)	CANTATE
TFL	FONTANA
7eg	HMV.
33CX	COLUMBIA